THE PHILIPPINES

Yesterday and Today

Delia and Ferdinand Kuhn

HOLT, RINEHART and WINSTON, Inc.

New York

Contemporary Civilizations Series

The motif on the title page and at the beginning of each chapter is a sun, symbolizing liberty, taken from the Philippine flag.

Grateful acknowledgment to reprint the following material is given to:

THE JOHN DAY COMPANY and HAROLD MATSON COMPANY for passages from Carlos P. Romulo's *Crusade in Asia*, Copyright © 1955 by Carlos P. Romulo.

FOREIGN AFFAIRS for passages from Wolf Ladejinsky's article, "Agrarian Reform in Asia," *Foreign Affairs*, April 1964.

HOUGHTON MIFFLIN COMPANY for passages from Volume II of Charles S. Olcott's *The Life of William McKinley*, Copyright 1916 by Houghton Mifflin Company.

INDIANA UNIVERSITY PRESS and LONGMANS, GREEN & COMPANY LIMITED for passages from Leon Guerrero's introduction to José Rizal's *The Lost Eden*, Copyright © 1961.

THE MACMILLAN COMPANY for passages from Francis Bowes Sayre's *Glad Adventure*, Copyright © 1957 by The Macmillan Company.

JOHN MURRAY LIMITED for passages from Sir John Bowring's *A Visit to the Philippine Islands*, Copyright 1859 by Smith, Elder & Company.

PHILIPPINES FREE PRESS for passages from "The Illusion of Amending the Constitution," *Philippines Free Press*, March 13, 1965.

NAJEEB M. SALEEBY for passages from Dr. Cesar Adib Majul's introduction to Saleeby's *History of Sulu*, Filipiniana Book Guild, Copyright © 1963.

TIME, INC. for passages from Volume I, page 277, *Memoirs of Harry S. Truman*, Doubleday & Company, Inc., Copyright © 1955 by Time, Inc.

Preface

Every generation needs to rewrite and rethink history. The present generation has a special opportunity and a special duty to do this, for it has watched the death of old empires, and the birth from their bodies of more than fifty new nation-states. It is thus the first generation that can define the problems of newly independent peoples and relate them to their colonial past.

The Philippines, which won independence from the United States in 1946, was the first of the new nations to achieve full political freedom after World War II. Its colonial past belongs to history; its first experience of full independence is ready for appraisal. Like their Southeast Asian neighbors, Filipinos have found this first experience baffling and sometimes painful. President Carlos P. Romulo of the University of the Philippines has called it a period of "decolonizing." The term offers clues to much that has been happening in Southeast Asia.

The present book seeks to interpret the Philippines' period of decolonizing in the light of its American, Spanish, and pre-Spanish past. The subject is far larger than this brief introductory study, and the authors can claim to have made only a modest start toward a comprehensive picture. They owe thanks to past chroniclers, American and Spanish, but primarily to modern Filipino writers and politicians, for throwing light on the trials and triumphs of the new republic.

DELIA AND FERDINAND KUHN have been traveling to Asia since 1951 to gather material for books and articles. Writing assignments took them to the Philippines in 1954, during the Magsaysay administration; in 1958, when they crossed the Sulu Sea in a gunboat from Mindanao to Borneo; and twice in 1964. They are co-authors of *Borderlands* (1962), a section of which deals with Mindanao and the Sulu islands. Mrs. Kuhn, a graduate of Vassar, was Associate Editor of *Current History*. She also served in the Federal Government for ten years as a writer and information officer. Mr. Kuhn, a Columbia University graduate, is a former London correspondent of *The New York Times*. He was deputy director of the Office of War Information, and wrote for the *Washington Post* for seven postwar years as its reporter on foreign affairs. He is the author of two books for young readers, *Commodore Perry and the Opening of Japan* and *The Story of the Secret Service*.

VERA MICHELES DEAN, general editor of the Contemporary Civilizations Series, is professor of international development at the Graduate School of Public Administration, New York University. Mrs. Dean was research director and editor of the Foreign Policy Association, 1928–1961, and served as director of the non-Western Civilizations Program at The University of Rochester, 1954–1962.

With the assistance of Harry D. Harootunian, Mrs. Dean prepared the anthology WEST AND NON-WEST: NEW PERSPECTIVES which is the basic reader in the Contemporary Civilizations Series.

Contents

THE PHILIPPINES

A LONE among the new nations of eastern Asia, the Philippines bears the lasting imprint of not one but two colonial regimes: those of Spain and the United States. The Spaniards infused their Roman Catholic faith into the simple animist society of the Islands; they imposed their centralized rule upon a fragmented people. They not only kept but strengthened ancient systems of land tenure and agriculture. And for 333 years they blanketed the Filipinos—"the Indians," as they called them—with European condescension, in the accepted imperial manner of the era. In Spanish eyes, the people of the Philippines were children who could never rule themselves.

The Americans conquered this Asian colony when it was in active rebellion, first against Spain and then against the

United States. Almost from the start, Americans interpreted their mission differently from the Spaniards. The Americans sought to train Filipinos for self-government, to introduce mass public education and public health, to superimpose industry on a traditional rural economy, and to exemplify American ideals of private initiative and public service. All these changes the Americans attempted without reforming the traditional social system. Their unconventional experiment in imperial rule, interrupted by the Japanese invasion, lasted until 1946.

With such contrasting experiences behind it, is it any wonder that the new Philippine Republic has no exact counterpart in Asia? On the one hand, as the distinguished writer-diplomat, Leon Guerrero, has said:

> The Filipinos, inspired by Rizal, made the first nationalist revolution in Asia in 1896, established its first democratic republic, which survived until 1901, and in 1946, exactly fifty years after Rizal's execution, became the first Asians to win independence from Western colonialism.

He could have added that the independent Republic has never known a dictator, has held to a democratic constitution, has transferred power only by constitutional means, and has cherished a free press, free speech, free enterprise, and a free political opposition.

At the same time, the Filipinos remain basically an Asian people. Their land and climate are Southeast Asian, their ethnic origin is Asian, and many of their social institutions remain Asian in spite of centuries of Western rule. That free institutions can thrive in such an environment is one of the marvels and mysteries of Southeast Asia. For these and other reasons, the Filipinos deserve the attention of the historian and the student of current affairs.

The Land

The Philippine Republic consists of more than 7,000 islands. The exact number at any moment depends on geological caprice, which occasionally pushes a volcanic peak above the sea or allows another to be washed under by the waves. The Islands are the northernmost links of the vast Malay chain, which half encircles Southeast Asia. They face the Asian mainland across the South China Sea at distances varying from 500 to 800 miles.

Like most of Southeast Asia, the Philippine Islands belong to the wet tropics—the warmest, wettest, and probably the richest portion of the earth. In their lush warmth, their scatteration, and their closeness to Asia, one can find clues to the character of the modern Philippine Republic and of its people.

Island Regions

It has not been easy to make a nation out of so many bits and pieces. Although its land area is equal only to that of Britain and Ireland taken together, its coastlines are longer than those of the United States. Forty-five islands contain the bulk of the land; eleven, the bulk of the people. About 1,000 are permanently settled.

The archipelago divides into four natural regions. One of these is the island of Luzon, which commands the whole archipelago by virtue of its size, wealth, population, and political leadership. Luzon is slightly larger than Cuba. It has the nation's historic capital, Manila, a metropolis of more than two million people. (The new official capital, Quezon City, is a Manila suburb.) It has Manila Bay, which is not only the nation's best seaport, but one of the world's most spacious harbors. It has the largest expanses of level farmland anywhere in the Philippines: the Great Central Plain and the fertile valleys of the Cagayan and Trinidad Rivers in the north. Luzon is crisscrossed by rugged mountain ranges, one rising to 8,000 feet. Yet its people lead the nation in rice, sugar, tobacco, and vegetable cultivation. The island boasts six-sevenths of the nation's scarce irrigated acres. It shelters more than a third of the 30 million Filipinos. In or near Manila are concentrated more than half the factories and industrial workers in the Philippines.

A second natural region is the land mass of Mindanao in the south. In sharp contrast to Luzon, Mindanao is compara-

In an island nation, boats are important. Here, a large outrigger is under construction on the island of Panay in the Visayas.

tively empty, unexplored, and untapped, although by 1965 it already held five million people. It is potentially the richest of all the islands. Here are concentrated most of the nation's resources for the future: uncut timber, unmined iron and nickel, unharnessed rivers, and large but dwindling pockets of unused farmland. Mindanao's sparse and mixed population already supplies the nation with much of its corn, coconut, abaca (hemp), and pineapple crops. The island's main port of Davao is the third largest in the country. With pioneer settlers always drifting in from Luzon and the Visayas to the north, Mindanao will have little time left to enjoy its wide empty spaces.

The overcrowded Visayas form a third region. This central cluster, separating Luzon from Mindanao, includes the economically important island of Cebu and five others of respectable size: Mindoro, Leyte, Negros, Samar, and Panay. The Visayans grow and eat most of the Philippine corn, which, next to rice, is the chief food crop of the nation. Visayans process much of the country's sugar cane. The city of Cebu, a provincial capital, is an industrial center and seaport second in importance only to Manila.

Southward from Mindanao, a miniature archipelago crosses the eastern end of the Sulu Sea like stepping stones to within sight of Borneo. In the western part of the Sulu Sea, another group of islands reaches toward Borneo from Mindoro. The largest of these islands, lizard-shaped Palawan, is physically an extension of Borneo, to which it was attached in prehistoric ages. Geographically, the islands on and around the Sulu Sea link the Philippines with the rest of the great chain. Historically, they were famous as trading and pearl fishing centers, as well as the first foothold of Islam in the Philippines. The Sulu islands remain a community of Muslims. In modern times they became a closed community, outside the mainstream of Philippine life and change. They form the least known and the most difficult to know of the four regions.

The idea of regionalism, growing logically out of the nation's fragmented form, has a firm hold on the Philippine consciousness. Island geography has promoted regional languages, cultures, and loyalties. The implications of these diversities for building and governing a nation will emerge in later chapters.

The Asian Links

The position of the Philippines, like that of Britain and other island nations, is ambivalent. They are part of the neighboring continent, yet separate from it. There is little doubt that the Philippine Islands were once physically connected with the Asian mainland, by way of the island chain of which they are the northern links. Moreover, they were peopled from Asia. Their climate, vegetation, and animals have more similarities than differences when compared with those of Southeast Asia. They face the Asian mainland to the west across the warm and comparatively shallow waters of the South China Sea.

By contrast, the Pacific Ocean at their backs is deep and wide. Geologists place the Philippines in the "fiery circle" of volcanic islands that rim the Pacific basin. And biologists recently settled a long argument by deciding to call the Philippines "transitional," because their flora and fauna show traces of Australian as well as Asian influences.

Yet the Asian links, both geographic and ethnic, are clearly the stronger. Asians migrating to the islands brought their rice culture, their mining of gold, their fishing of the seas and inland waters, their languages and early religions,

their patterns of trade, their uses of land. Thus it was the
Asian links which for thousands of years shaped and dictated
the character and life of the Philippines. Then, suddenly, in
the course of a hundred years, events intervened to reverse
the logic of geography.

In the sixteenth century, navigators from Europe "discovered" the vast island chain. They called it the "Indies,"
assuming it to be somehow an extension of India. Of the
competing Europeans, it was the Spaniards who laid claim to
the 7,000 bits and pieces at the northern extreme of the
chain. They gave their prize the name "Philippines" in honor
of their King Philip the Second. Henceforth, for almost 400
years, the Philippine archipelago and its peoples turned their
backs on Asia. Conquerors came to them first from Spain,
then from Spanish Mexico, and finally from the United
States. The conquerors broke the islands' long associations
with Asian trade, peoples and cultures. In their place, they
forged new links with Europe and North America. They
tried, with considerable success, to superimpose their Western cultures on those of the Asian islanders. Not until 1946
did Filipinos recover the opportunity to redress the balance
of geography. With independence came the possibility of
turning once more to the Asia of their neighborhood and
their past.

~The Wet Tropics

What are the physical traits which the Philippines share with
their Southeast Asian neighbors? Three traits are common to
the whole area: all of it is warm, rain-fed, and immensely
rich in the bounties of nature. These wet Asian tropics,
in startling contrast with other tropics of the Middle
East and Africa, do not know the meaning of deserts and

droughts. In this part of Asia the growing season is twelve months long. Rain falls somewhere in the Philippines every day in the year, carried by the northeast trade winds in the winter, the southwest monsoon in the summer. Rain is not only plentiful (from 60 to 300 inches annually) but reliable, year in, year out. This does not mean, however, that it is everywhere evenly distributed throughout the year. In about one-fourth of the Philippine land area there are so-called dry months in which less than three inches of rain falls. These regions are usually to the west of mountain ranges which shield them from the rain-bearing northeast trades. Dry periods, however, are offset by seasons of rainfall from the southeast.

The Philippines has a north-south span of more than eleven hundred miles. Yet the northernmost island, within sight of Formosa, is no colder than the southernmost, on Borneo's doorstep. At sea level, the heat rarely reaches 100°. The coldest temperature ever officially recorded was 60°—at an altitude of 4,860 feet. It is altitude, not latitude, which accounts for such variations as there are.

A glance at a topographical map shows why variations occur. Mountains dominate the Philippine landscape. An aerial view reveals "the evergreen islands which rise in endless clusters on the smooth seas of the Malayan Archipelago," as Sir Stamford Raffles, the great British proconsul, described the Indies. The mountains jut out of the seas in spiny ridges, rimmed with narrow coastal plains. Only a few of the Philippines are big enough to accommodate broad inland valleys and grassy plateaus between the ranges. But in these tropical mountains, which occasionally rise to 9,000 feet, extreme cold is as rare as extreme heat is in the lowlands.

However, the wet tropics are not always benign. In the Philippines, at least, nature betrays a Jekyll-Hyde personality,

The most famous of Philippine volcanoes is Mt. Mayon in southern Luzon. Its perfect cone, 7,943 feet high, dominates the village and bay below.

alternately pampering and punishing the land and its people. Between July and November, tropical typhoons regularly hit the northern half of the archipelago. During the summer months the Visayas and southern Luzon take the brunt of the storms; in the autumn northern Luzon becomes the victim. Mindanao and the Sulu islands lie just outside the typhoon trail and are thus the only islands of the Philippines where tall crops such as coconuts, corn, and abaca can thrive with immunity.

Approaching from the southeast, and moving west and northwest, typhoons are apt to strike the Philippines with 100-mile-an-hour winds, and to dump twenty inches of rain on one target in twenty-four hours. The resulting floods add to the chaos and destruction of crops, roads, bridges, and villages.

Volcanoes are among the wonders and terrors of the Philippines. One, on Luzon, sits in the middle of a lake; another, on the island of Jolo in the Sulu Archipelago, cradles a lake in its crater. Perhaps twenty are believed to be still active, among them Mount Apo, the highest peak in the archipelago. Philippine history is punctuated with eruptions which buried entire communities on surrounding slopes, in the manner of Vesuvius.

Natural Wealth

The fury of typhoons, volcanoes, and floods has left few scars on the land. This is because a quiet frenzy of growth quickly covers the wounds. The Philippines owes at least part of its extravagant natural wealth to the constant warmth and plentiful rains. People born in the wet tropics tend to take this extravagance for granted. But a visitor from tropical deserts or from temperate zones stands in wonder and disbelief at the speed and lushness of growth and the ease of human life on these islands. This wonder pervades the diaries of the explorers, naturalists, colonizers, and traders who have come upon the Philippines over the centuries.

A sizable part of the Philippines' natural wealth stands in its forests which now, after centuries of plunder and misuse, clothe less than half of the land. At sea level, dense mangrove swamps yield wood for building and burning, for charcoal and tanbark. Lofty rain forests overrun the foothills

Choked by the lush growth, a river in central Luzon threads its way through a rain forest.

with layer upon layer of green canopies, rising to 200 feet and shutting out the sun's rays; creepers garland the branches; bamboos, canes, mosses, and ferns carpet the forest floor. So dense is the growth, the United States Army advised soldiers, that in rain forests "it is generally possible to walk at the rate of one mile per hour." On higher and drier slopes, the trees thin out and shed their leaves. Scarce and valuable pines are found on Luzon and Mindoro, and on the partly unexplored island of Palawan.

Like the forests, the farmlands of the Philippines hide untold commercial rewards. In the process of cultivating about one-fourth of their land area, Filipinos have allowed their soils to be ravaged by erosion, by leaching, and by bad management. Still, under the right conditions, the land could grow almost every kind of tropical food and fibre in abundance. It has never failed to yield an unlimited variety. Among scores of fruits, for example, no fewer than sixty kinds of bananas flourish here. Edible roots, vegetables, cocoa, coffee, peanuts, cotton, and rubber are just a few of the minor crops. The most important crops for domestic consumption are rice and corn; those for export: sugar, coconuts, tobacco, and abaca. (See pp. 145–50.)

Rice tops the list of essential crops, for the majority of the people subsist on it. They plant it on half the cultivated land and on almost every inhabited island, but most intensively on the fertile central plain of Luzon. The economics of rice will be explored in a later chapter (see pp. 155–57), but it should be noted here that the yield of Philippine rice per acre is one of the lowest in the world. This goes far toward explaining why one of the most richly endowed of all agricultural nations does not manage to feed itself.

In addition to forests and farms, grasslands are extensive, covering between 15 and 20 per cent of the islands. Where hillsides have been stripped or fields abandoned by farmers, tough grasses often take over. Although unproductive and hard to uproot, they render, at any rate, one service: that of stopping erosion of the precious soil.

A third source of Philippine wealth, in addition to forests and farmlands, lurks in the warm waters that flow around and between the islands. According to expert estimates, Filipinos have access to about 2,000 types of edible fish. Many are in coastal waters, many others in the numerous rivers, brackish swamps, flooded rice fields, and homemade fish ponds. Not far outside their territorial waters lie rich tuna grounds, waiting to be tapped. And their own Sulu Sea

is famous for pearl oysters, as well as for huge marine turtles.

Fish ranks next to rice and corn as an essential food item. It is the main source of protein, which the Philippine diet generally lacks. Fresh fish is both scarce and expensive, and most Filipinos eat it salted, dried, and smoked. Since the commercial supply does not meet demand, fish, like rice, is on the list of imports.

A mountain land with plenty of rainfall and many rivers, the Philippines has never been short of water resources; but, ironically, the islanders are often short of water. A distinguished geographer, Robert S. Huke, remarks that where rainfall is concentrated in a few months, "huge volumes of water are allowed to escape to the sea unused during the wet season and only a small portion of the much reduced dry season flow is utilized." Moreover, only one acre of cultivated land in nine receives irrigation water. About five out of six of the irrigated acres are on the island of Luzon, in systems which have been built over the years since independence.

Many rivers are well suited to harnessing for flood control and electric power, as well as for irrigation. Two ambitious projects are under way: one in northern Mindanao, the other in central Luzon. Altogether, the Philippines has twenty-three hydroelectric plants in operation, and seventeen new ones are planned for construction by 1973. The fast-growing cities and most of the towns have been electrified. But for two-thirds of the people, those who live in rural areas, electricity remains out of reach. Their best hope of eventually

Lumberjacks felling a tree on Mindanao. Export of logs and lumber have more than tripled since 1940.

Salt deposits on Luzon—part of the mineral wealth in the Philippine mountains.

gaining cheap electric light and power in their villages and homes would seem to depend primarily on the development of their plentiful hydroelectric resources. The dream of oil, so richly available to neighboring Borneo, has faded.

Although oil and natural gas seem to be lacking, there is mineral wealth in the mountains of the Philippines. How much, and how exploitable, is not yet known. True stories of gold deposits in Luzon attracted Chinese traders more than a thousand years ago. The Spaniards were deeply disappointed with what they found, but the Americans later put the gold to good use to help the colony's balance of payments. Modern mining concentrates on moderate amounts of copper, chromite, and iron, all for export. The richest known but still untapped resources are iron and nickel ores in northeast Mindanao and islands off its coast. Their development, together with the rest of Mindanao's latent wealth, will depend upon the skills and enterprise of Filipinos yet unborn.

What the Land Offers

The wet tropics of Southeast Asia offer subsistence at a bargain price. Their people can satisfy their basic needs for food, shelter, and clothing with a comparatively small expenditure of time and energy. Most of them live at subsistence level. Of this generalization, the Philippines offers a prime example.

A Filipino family can feed itself on rice, root vegetables, and fruit without working many days in the week or many weeks in the year. This does not mean that it is well nourished, merely that it is fed. A Filipino family can shelter itself with three trees that grow almost everywhere: the coconut and nipa palms and the bamboo. These provide the supports, floors, walls, and roof of a house, as well as its furniture and many useful household articles. Usually they cost the family nothing. Most Filipinos do not need to cover themselves for warmth, but such clothing as custom requires them to wear is easy to make at home. They inherit, breed, and keep domestic animals at no cost. All this is possible at the subsistence level. It means that they are ill-nourished, but otherwise better off than people who merely subsist in the dry tropics or in cold climates.

The subsistence farmer with his plow.

The basic fact about subsistence is the total lack of surplus. From the sum of the farmer's labor nothing is left over. He cannot save to meet ordinary problems such as illness and inability to work; expenses of family weddings and funerals; disasters such as droughts, pests, and crop failures. Moreover, he cannot amass a bit of capital to replace a worn-out harrow or a dead water buffalo. To meet these familiar needs of rural people the world over, the subsistence farm family must go into debt to a landlord or a moneylender. Interest on the debt alone would be likely to absorb any surplus the farmer might earn in a good crop year. Debt is an unrelenting burden which wipes out the chance to get ahead, or to move from one's home. It thus imposes a kind of servitude, or at least a static life without freedom of choice. (See page 160.)

In addition, subsistence farming is inevitably destructive to the land. The farmer lacks the time to let his field lie fallow, the money to enrich it with fertilizer, the knowledge and skill to rotate his crops. All he can do is to take subsistence from the soil, year after year, so as to keep himself and his family alive.

In recent years much thought and energy have gone into the twin problem of how to lift the rural Philippines out of the vicious circle of subsistence, and how to rescue the bountiful land from erosion and slow destruction.

The People

Most of the 30 million modern Filipinos owe their origins to migrants from the Asian mainland. These migrants came to the Islands in countless waves over some fifty-five centuries. They were seaborne with one exception: the oldest known arrivals, the aborigines, who are believed to have walked over prehistoric land bridges from the mainland.

The long, slow process of assimilation produced a modern Filipino blend of Mongoloid and Caucasian, including Chinese and Japanese, Hindu, Persian, and Arab, and finally, European stock. Who the early migrants were, where they came from and when they came are questions to which scholars are still seeking definitive answers. On the following outlines of the nation's epic there would seem to be a measure of agreement.

Origins

The aborigines may have arrived on foot some 25,000 years ago. Their descendants can be found today in the deep forests of Luzon, Palawan, and lesser islands. Once numerous, they have dwindled to less than 1 per cent of the population. They are fully developed pygmies, less than five feet tall. Because of their coppery skins, kinky hair, broad noses, and thick lips, they have been called "Negritos." But there is no hard evidence to connect them with the pygmies of Africa or to indicate where they originated. They have not advanced beyond the hunting and gathering of food. They live in small units of a few families, without tribes, chieftains, or a language of their own. They have been the subject of many studies, on the assumption that their days are numbered.

Among the modern Filipinos' ancestors who came by sea, scholars have identified a number of ethnic types. The earliest of these was probably a Stone Age man who may have shoved his wooden boat from the Asian mainland as long as six thousand years ago. This pioneer was relatively tall and slender, with light brown skin and an aquiline nose. It is possible that he came by way of Formosa and approached Luzon from the north.

The second distinct type is thought to have been an Iron Age man. He could have launched his frail bark from the Asian mainland some 3,500 years after the Stone Age visitor. The newcomer was inclined to be short and stocky, with darker skin, thicker lips and a larger nose. In his later migrations, perhaps 500 years before Christ, he may have brought with him the art of terracing and irrigating mountain slopes for rice cultivation.

Scholars have speculated that in its deep past this branch of the family could have filtered into South and Southeast Asia by way of the great rivers which rise in the region of

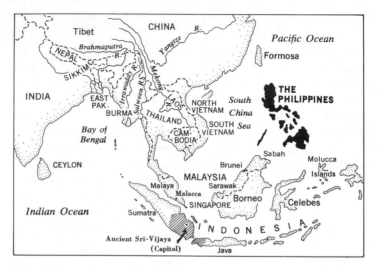

The Philippines' Asian Neighbors

Tibet. These, of course, include the Brahmaputra, the Irra-
waddy, the Salween, the Mekong, and the Yangtze. Such a
theory takes into account a strange resemblance between the
skilled rice engineers of Luzon in the Philippines, the Nagas
of northeastern India, and the Karens of Burma. It suggests
also their possible kinship with the terraced-rice farmers of
Nepal and Sikkim in the Himalayas.

We come now to the third and most important migrant-
ancestor of today's Philippine man: the Malay. The physical
traits of the Malay include brown skin, medium height, and
straight black hair. This man made his long and leisurely
way from the Asian mainland with stopovers in Sumatra or
Borneo or other islands to the south and west of his eventual
home. Beginning about three centuries before Christ and

continuing for more than a thousand years, waves of Malays filtered through the island chain, acquiring strains of Persian and Indian blood which are still evident in the modern blend. So strong is the Malay infusion into the Philippine ethnic complex that "Malay blend" has become a common and convenient, if oversimplified, term to describe the people of the Philippines.

The present-day homeland of the Malays stretches from the Malay Peninsula on the mainland through the necklace of some 10,000 islands once called the "Indies." In twentieth-century political terms, they inhabit the republics of Indonesia, the Philippines, Singapore and the Federation of Malaysia. They speak many versions of the same language. Nevertheless, it is possible for a Tagalog-speaker on the island of Luzon to find linguistic affinities with a Sumatran and a mainland Malay.

Other infusions should be noted for their importance rather than their size. It is estimated that one Filipino in ten is either all or part Chinese, the product of infiltration from mainland China for more than a thousand years. Finally, the combined Spanish and American components affect perhaps 3 per cent of the modern mosaic. It would be difficult to find a leading Filipino family which does not show one or both of these elements.

Ethnic Character

Whether the 30 million Filipinos of today should be regarded as a blend or a mosaic depends upon one's point of view. As distinguished a historian as Joseph Ralston Hayden, writing just before World War II, insisted that it was their homogeneity rather than their diversity which was "the outstanding fact about the Filipino people." To support his

*These villagers from an island in the Sulu Archipelago are
fair examples of the "Malay blend."*

thesis that they had the makings of a nation, he argued that
"in blood and ancestry they are at least as unified as are the
inhabitants of Great Britain, France, Spain, or the United
States."

More convincing is the abundant evidence of diversity
assembled by the leading ethnologist in the Philippines,
Professor H. Otley Beyer. He has identified no fewer than

forty-five different "ethnographic groups," each consisting of people "who have sufficiently unique economic and social life, language, or physical type to mark them off clearly and distinctly from any other similar group in the Philippine Islands." Moreover, Professor Beyer counted sixty dialects and seven major languages possessing printed literatures. Authorities differ on the number of groups and tongues, but they agree in general on the vastly varied character of the ethnic mosaic. They point out that within its framework, one can find and study almost all the stages of man's cultural ascent from the Stone to the Atomic Age. For this among other reasons, it is not surprising that the Philippines have become known as treasure islands.

Philippine geography has helped to preserve and shape the ethnic mosaic. In spite of live volcanoes, earthquakes, and typhoons, the islands are warmly hospitable to human life and survival. They float on the tropical sea like some 7,000 sponges, absorbing the waves of humanity that wash onto their shores. Except for one martial group, the Muslims or "Moros" of the southern islands, who would rather fight than flee, rather die than adapt, settlers who found themselves in danger from a new oncoming wave would take to their boats and move to another island. Or they would take to the hinterland by way of numerous river valleys. They did not need to flee far for sanctuary. In nearby forests, mountain valleys, or fertile plateaus they could keep their individual cultures relatively intact, and, if necessary, adapt them to new conditions. The terrain of the islands is ideal for these purposes.

As one example of many, it has been suggested that the northern Luzon rice terraces might in fact constitute such an adaptation. The accepted theory has assumed that these highly skilled techniques of carving the mountainsides and

channeling water down them were imported from the Asian mainland perhaps 500 years before Christ. Could they not have been a triumphant adaptation by lowland rice farmers fleeing from Spanish conquest in the sixteenth century? A curious fact is cited to support this new thesis: so spectacular an engineering feat went unmentioned throughout the records of pre-Spanish times.

Americans are familiar with the ways in which geography encourages isolation and consequent diversity. Even now there are American Indians of prehistoric cultures clinging to narrow ledges of the Grand Canyon. And until recently a good many Kentucky mountain folk were able to preserve a language akin to Shakespeare's. Some Filipinos likewise continue to defy the miracles of modern communication and to show how overrated they can be as blenders of mankind.

Those Filipinos who fled to isolation have paid the usual price for it. Their numbers are dwindling. Only a few can still be called authentically primitive. These include the aboriginal pygmies and some descendants of the first sea-borne immigrants. They rove in the deep forests of Luzon, Mindanao, Palawan, and some of the larger Visayas, hunting small game with bows and arrows, and sometimes hunting one another.

On a more skilled and organized level are upland farmers of dry rice and root vegetables and keepers of pigs and chickens. They build bamboo huts and move only when the hillsides they have cultivated are no longer fertile. Their methods of slashing and burning the vegetation in prepara-

The Philippine population is often called a mosaic because the Islands shelter so many groups that have preserved distinct ways of life. These people are members of a tribe of sea gypsies who ply the waters off eastern Mindanao.

The famed rice terraces of northern Luzon.

tion for sowing dry rice and other crops has caused wide-spread erosion and loss of precious soil. It is estimated that 60,000 such farmers annually strip more than 100,000 acres of woodland. This practice is today a burning issue in more than one sense. Appeals and warnings from the Philippine government have fallen on deaf ears; the slash-and-burn farmers either do not understand or do not intend to change their ways. Except to foresters, soil conservationists, and scholars who seek them out for study, these upland peoples are little known.

On still another level are the rice terracers of northern Luzon. Despite their fame, they are relatively withdrawn. Their culture remained alive, yet they somehow got lost to the outer world for centuries and then were rediscovered. Whoever were the people who sculpted the mountainsides, irrigated them, and grew rice at from 1,500 to 5,000 feet, they were first of all great earth movers. They were, secondly, skilled engineers. They were, thirdly, remarkable stone masons. And they were, finally, clever social innovators, for they fashioned a system of communal labor and water use that seems to have served their needs through the ages.

The forest and mountain peoples we have mentioned have eluded both Christian and Muslim missionaries. Like their ancestors, they go on worshiping, fearing, and placating spirits. They have managed also to remain largely impervious to the successive authorities of Spain, the United States, and even the Republic of the Philippines. With some exceptions, they have avoided becoming museum exhibits like Japan's Ainu and America's Indians in the national parks.

We come now to the last and largest of the isolationist groups: the Muslim minorities of Mindanao and the Sulu Archipelago. Other factors from those we have described have combined to keep them apart. They are the traditional seafaring and fighting peoples of the Islands. They were not only fierce warriors but also master sailors, fishermen, traders, pirates, and slave gatherers. The first of the islanders to be converted to the Muslim faith, they developed a religious pride and a fanatical loyalty to Islam. Spaniards who came to Christianize and rule the islands found the Muslims of Mindanao and Sulu to be the only peoples united

This man and his people farm the northern Luzon rice terraces. He is carving with the Filipino knife known as a bolo.

in their resistance by something like a national consciousness. Spain never wholly subdued them.

These "Moros," as the Spaniards called them, were the most dangerous of their Filipino subjects. They were also furthest from Manila, the center of Spanish power. Thus geography served the Moro minority well in preserving its integrity and its Muslim way of life.

We have seen how various minorities stayed outside the mainstream of Philippine life, thus keeping their identities relatively intact. What about the majority of Filipinos, concentrated on the coastal plains where they are easily accessible? These are the people who accepted the Christian faith and Spanish rule with only sporadic resistance. Yet even they have survived as "ethnographic groups," as Dr. Beyer has called the pieces of the mosaic. Consider, for example, three major groups, the Ilocanos, Tagalogs, and Cebuanos, each with its own language, each credited with its own special character.

The 3 million Ilocanos thickly populate a narrow strip of coast in northwest Luzon. Known as a hardworking, aggressive people, they are sometimes called the Scots, sometimes the Yankees, of the Philippines. Overcrowding, poor soil, and Chinese admixture are among the reasons cited for their toughness, reserve, and thrift. Yet Ilocanos have migrated widely through the Islands without seeming loss of these qualities.

In contrast, the neighboring Tagalogs are regarded as the most pleasure-loving, easygoing, and volatile of Filipinos. Outnumbering Ilocanos two to one, they have contributed the basis for a national language, as well as much music, art, and literature. They cultivate irrigated rice land in Luzon and have developed the most concentrated area of Philippine industries and handicrafts in and around Manila.

To the south of Luzon, in the Visayas, we meet the Cebuanos. They, with their neighboring Visayans, outnumber every other "ethnographic group," with about a quarter of the entire Philippine population. Cebuanos have preserved their own language and literature, with many related dialects.

From their crowded island of Cebu they have gone out as pioneers to other Visayan islands and to northern Mindanao. Wherever they settle, they grow and eat corn, the second largest food crop in the Philippines. And however dispersed, they are said to feel an almost tribal loyalty and an allegiance to their capital city, Cebu. A large and thriving port, second only to Manila, Cebu is known for its processing of foods, cement, and fertilizer.

Foreign Influence

How did the Ilocanos, the Tagalogs, the Cebuanos, and other Christian groups maintain their individual identities through so many generations of foreign domination? The year 1965 marked the four-hundredth anniversary of the beginning of Spanish rule. For all but twenty of those 400 years, Filipinos were in the custody of alien powers: Spain, the United States, and Japan. No people in the Far East has experienced so long a continuous colonial impact. The Spaniards imposed a new religion and a single authority, the first the islanders had known. The Americans brought authority of a different kind, a new ethic, and values that were little short of revolutionary. Through it all, the Filipinos cherished their individualities, nurtured their local enmities, and did what they could to salvage their traditions.

The psychology of subject peoples, their reactions to alien rule and to change, remain highly conjectural subjects of study by anthropologists and social scientists. One theory,

A Muslim of the southern Philippines. His turban is a relic of early Indian influence; his knife is the traditional weapon.

*In boats like these Muslim sailors fish the waters around
Mindanao and the Sulu Archipelago.*

developed by Filipino scholars, maintains that the islanders
were highly selective in their reactions. As each colonial
regime descended on them like a blanket of snow, they
seemed to absorb what least offended their traditions and
their temperament. What they could not or would not absorb
they bore as an unavoidable burden or tried to reject. Thus
the peace they made with their conquerors was usually short
of full surrender.

From the Spaniards the Filipinos absorbed Roman Catholicism into their inherited spirit worship, and the Spanish
clergy constantly complained of the admixture. The village
chieftains accepted Spanish overlordship and in return were
allowed to keep their hereditary powers plus the authority to
collect taxes. On the other hand, Spanish rule reluctantly

goaded Filipinos, who were separatists at heart, into a national consciousness. The Spaniards exacted forced labor and tribute. When local groups found these demands unreasonable and harsh, they rose in sporadic, fruitless rebellions. What finally persuaded most of them to hang together was the 300-year experience of hanging separately. Thus Spain's blunders inadvertently sowed the seeds of revolution and unity; the American takeover, in its turn, was to prepare the Filipinos for self-government and eventual nationhood.

Some of the leading Filipinos who rebelled against Spain in 1896 had been educated in Europe. From Western Europe's more advanced countries, they absorbed ideas of civil rights and mass secular education. These ideas they took back and incorporated into their abortive rebel constitution, so that the Philippines might also become an "advanced" country. Although the illiterate majority had no experience with education, the word took on magic connotations, promising deliverance from poverty and servitude. This helped the American teacher, whether a sweaty soldier or a Boston schoolmarm, to gain acceptance, as a symbol of potential dignity and eventual freedom.

Only among the Muslim communities (the pagans being largely out of reach of American teachers) did public education meet passive resistance. It was on mainly religious grounds: children's schooling that was not based on the law, customs, and moral precepts of the Koran was unacceptable.

Today Filipinos are undoubtedly among the most passionately education-oriented of newly independent peoples. Even the Muslims, as we shall see, are attending a state university specially designed to integrate Christian and Muslim students in the Muslim stronghold of Mindanao.

Filipinos likewise took to training for self-government, which the United States quickly introduced. The Americans attached their own national ethic to government service: that

public office is a public trust. To this American ideal, too often disregarded in the United States itself, Filipino politicians gave enthusiastic lip service, and still do. Yet it would be difficult to find a society in which the pretense of honest government is so lavish, the performance so meager. The traditional value of service to one's kinsmen continues to take precedence over service to the public. Too many Filipino public servants regard their offices as instruments of the higher good, namely, service to their families. In short, Filipinos show selectivity in the fashioning of their political institutions. The extent to which they have clung to traditional and Spanish patterns on the one hand, while adapting American patterns on the other, is detailed in Chapter V.

Acceptance of mass education led to remarkable changes in some fields. For example, the position of women altered radically under American tutelage. (See pages 186–89.) Another phenomenon was the swift development of mechanical skills compared with the slower pace of other Southeast Asian colonies. Americans introduced young Filipinos to the gasoline engine. As a result of early acquaintance and aptitude, skilled Filipinos were able to make good use of jeeps and other surplus equipment left behind after World War II. Thus they have earned a reputation as the best trained mechanics of the region. Skilled Filipinos are probably less averse to working with their hands than any other East Asians except for the Japanese.

Many of the inhabitants of Luzon are neither Ilocano nor Tagalog. This man is from the same province as former President Macapagal. He is weaving palm-stem fiber into rope.

The Philippine reputation extends also to medicine. By Southeast Asian standards, Filipino doctors, nurses, and pharmacists are numerous and highly proficient. As in other countries, they tend to huddle in cities. But under the Philippine "Operation Brotherhood," volunteer medical teams have gone out to serve in the jungles of Vietnam and Laos. Filipinos are not the only examples in Asia of skilled men who enlist for overseas adventure more readily than for service in their own rural slums.

Examples of resistance to change are numerous, and they are by no means confined to the less educated Filipinos. While the ignorant tenant farmer clings to ancient practices of tilling the rice field, his well-schooled landlord, often university-trained, uses his influence and wealth to block reform of the antiquated system of land tenancy. (See pages 159–60.) In his primary occupation, agriculture, the Filipino has a reputation of being among the least progressive and least efficient in Southeast Asia. How and where the average Filipino lives may throw some light on this problem.

The Average Filipino

Within the Philippine mosaic, it is possible to find and depict the "average" person. In this context, "average" means the three out of four islanders who do not live in cities or lurk in the forests. It means the rural, Christian majority. Of these, a few are lonely homesteaders; most live in small towns, comparable to American county seats, or in *barrios*.

The *barrio* is the Philippine village. Several clusters of homes usually make up a *barrio*. From these homes farmers, and at certain times their families, go out to work in the surrounding fields. The homes and fields are connected by dirt roads, cart tracks, or footpaths. A *barrio* is almost certain to have a general so-called *sari-sari* store. There are more

A barrio *housewife in central Luzon does her laundry near the pure water well.*

than 100,000 such stores in the 18,000 or so *barrios*. Their stocks vary, but they usually include soft drinks, pots and pans, sweets, and cotton yard goods. The store is one social center; the coeducational elementary school is another. Often the school was built by local labor and subscription, on the promise of a teacher from the government. As the focal point of the community, the school may get more use than the Roman Catholic chapel, with its non-resident visiting priest.

Barrio women congregate daily at the *barrio* water source, be it a well, a pond, or a stream, to bathe, do their laundry, hear the news, and fill water jugs for domestic use. The heart of the *barrio* is the individual family home: a detached square house, standing on stilts from five to eight feet above ground. The family built it of local materials: wood or bamboo posts, woven bamboo walls, palm or thatch roof. Its two or three rooms are surrounded by wide open porches. Access is by ladder, which can be drawn up at any time. Under the house there is dry storage space for tools, a farm cart, and perhaps a loom.

The *barrio* house is well suited to the climate and way of life. It has not changed much over the centuries. It is cheap and easy to build; it can be kept clean and ventilated. Depending on care and climate, it will last perhaps fifteen years. While the style of the house has not changed much, the contents have. In addition to the old clay stove, cooking pots, water jars, straw mats, and kapok pillows, there now are likely to be furniture, oil lamps, a mirror, a crucifix, framed family pictures, perhaps a radio, and an old-fashioned sewing machine. The yard would almost surely contain a pig-pen, chickens running loose, and flowers in profusion. The potted plant, sometimes hanging from the roof or porch railing, denotes family pride and love of decoration.

An average Filipino family under one roof may number seven or eight persons, four or five of them children under fifteen years old. The third adult is a relative who may be old, ill, or unemployed. It is probable that the whole family was born in the *barrio,* and that it owns the house but not the land beneath it.

The average family farms the land around the *barrio* under one of several conditions. The farmer may be a tenant,

To barrio *women like these, the sewing machine has long been a status symbol.*

The carabao's *main job is to pull the harrow or plow in the flooded rice field.*

paying rent in crops or money; he may be a hired hand on an estate; he may be an independent farmer-owner. If he is the last, his holding is probably less than five acres, his crop yield is low, and he runs short of food from one harvest to the next. Yet he is better off than the tenant farmer who rarely gets out of debt to his landlord. (See pages 18–19 and 160.) The plight of the landless hired hand may be still worse; for in addition to earning low wages, he can be laid off by the landlord.

Secondary sources of income and food are available to the average family. Among these, hogs, bananas, and fish ponds are the most common. Others include home industries making straw mats, hats, baskets, and brooms. Indispensable family tools are the knife, called a *bolo,* and the *carabao,* or water buffalo. The Philippine *carabao* is a beast of many virtues: strong, slow, and reliable, if sometimes stubborn. For slogging through the mud of a flooded rice field, he has no rival. The farmer drives his *carabao* to the field at dawn; they work together until ten; then they rest until two, and work again until sunset. The *carabao* cannot stand working through the noonday heat.

In spite of these long hours, the average Filipino finds time for recreation. The family has its own festivals, with dancing, singing, and guitar playing. Saint's-day *fiestas* bring out the whole *barrio* for processions with religious images, candles, flowers, balloons, fireworks, and brass bands. Manly recreation includes the almost universal Sunday cockfight.

For both sexes, politics and voting have become a favorite diversion. Ebullient spirits, love of talk, and music tend to mask the depth of *barrio* poverty. When General Carlos P. Romulo campaigned for the presidency in remote *barrios* in 1953 (he withdrew from the race before the election), he saw to his shock and horror the underlying misery of a poor farmer's daily life. He spent a typical campaigning night

> . . . in the shack of a peasant, huddled on the floor under a leaky roof by the light of a guttering candle or small oil lamp, around a fire of carabao dung, sharing by use of the fingers the family dish of boiled rice with a sprinkle of salt, with the added delicacies perhaps of crude molasses or a dried salted fish, caught in the nearby river. For the night ahead there loomed the prospect of broken sleep in this crowded hut, where perhaps fourteen persons shared a room, not counting the family's meager supply of livestock. . . So the Filipino in the remote barrios had lived for centuries. So he was living still, in this year 1953.

The average Filipino is born, bears children, and dies without medical care. Usually he must travel to the nearest municipal center to find a doctor or a hospital. Few *barrios* are equipped with electricity, mail service, newspapers, or telephones.

In short, the physical impact on the *barrio* of nearly 400

years of Western rule has been slight. The houses, the landscape, the people are startlingly reminiscent of what Magellan's companion, Antonio Pigafetta, saw in the coastal settlements of the sixteenth century, and what nineteenth-century travelers described. There are, of course, some new kinds of buildings since Magellan's day: the Roman Catholic church or chapel, the general store, the schoolhouse, and, more recently, the village sanitary latrine.

In the same way it is still possible to discern the outlines of the old social structure which the Spaniards found and preserved. A hereditary chieftain, or *datu,* presided over the village, or *barangay.* His subjects were divided into three classes: the freeborn, who tilled a piece of the communally-owned land and kept their crops, but contributed feudal-type services to the ruling family; the serfs, who forfeited half their crops to the chieftain; and the "slaves," or indentured laborers, who lived on his estate and were his property. The traditional chieftain corresponds in very general terms to the modern *cacique,* who is a large landowner or political boss wielding great local power. The freeborn might be compared with modern farm owners, the serfs with modern share-croppers, the "slaves" with landless laborers of today.

One fundamental new fact dwarfs these apparent similarities. It is political. The modern *barrio* man and woman vote in national and, recently, in local elections. The humblest villager has a potential voice. (See pages 132 and 141–42.)

Much has been written about the *tao,* the common man of the *barrios.* Filipino and even American scholars like to picture the *tao* as a dumb beast of burden, mired like his *carabao* in ignorance. From this image those with first-hand acquaintance of the *barrio* Filipino must dissent. More than a hundred years ago Sir John Bowring, the British colonial governor of Hong Kong, wrote that he did not believe in the "invincible inertness" of this man. Bowring judged the

The luxury of a modern apartment in Manila is beyond the means of most Filipinos.

"Indians" of the Philippines, as they were then called, to be capable of initiative and managerial skill, "when they are properly encouraged." He cited examples such as this one:

> I heard of a native in one of the most distant villages I visited in Panay, who had been recommended by a friar to take to sugar-growing. He did so, and obtained five hundred dollars for the produce which he for the first time took down to Iloilo. He will get a thousand the second year. A little additional labor produces so much that the smallest impulse gives great results, especially where employed over a vast extent.

Bowring, however, noted that individual enterprise of this kind needed two prerequisites for success. First, the farmer must have possession of his land "absolutely and irrevocably secured to him"; and, second, "once installed by the government he must be protected against all molestation of his title." For these conditions the *tao* is still waiting, a century

after Bowring. Bowring's judgment is corroborated by men and women whose work has been to encourage initiative in the *barrios*. Yet the image of "invincible inertness" persists.

It comes, in the main, from a minority which has isolated itself no less effectively than the forest dwellers—the urban elite. Between them and the average Filipino of the *barrio* there is a gap in understanding and communication. In recent decades this gap has grown wider as modern—meaning Western—ideas and techniques poured into the cities and merely trickled into the rural countryside.

The Philippine urban minority is rather large, as compared with countries in the rest of Southeast Asia. It accounts for perhaps 10 or 12 per cent of the total population and is growing fast. Metropolitan Manila alone is believed to shelter two and a half million souls. Here are concentrated the wealthiest and the poorest people in the nation. Sometimes they live side by side, a shanty in the shadow of a mansion. More often they occupy separate districts walled off from each other by fear and resentment. It is in these urban centers, Manila, Davao, Cebu, and others, that the rapid population growth of the Philippines is most obvious and is causing the deepest concern.

Population Growth

A word of caution should preface any discussion of population. "The vital statistics of the Philippines are grossly defective," concluded a joint study by the United Nations and the Philippine government, published in 1960. This study explained that many births and deaths are never registered. Other obstacles, such as multiple languages and poor

A street scene in one of Manila's poorer districts.

communications, stand in the way of an accurate nationwide census.

Demographic experts, however, are in general agreement on the following points. With about 30 million people, in the middle of the 1960's, the Philippine Islands are not overcrowded. Overall population density is about one-third that of Japan and not quite double that of the United States. This is not to say that people are evenly distributed or well supplied with land, work, or food. They are not.

Demographers express concern not about the size of the population, but about the rate at which it is growing. This rate, reflecting the excess of births over deaths, is believed to be about 3 per cent a year, and is one of the highest rates in the world. It has not always been so high. Between the censuses of 1903 and 1918, the average annual rate of growth was just under 2 per cent. By the census of 1939, it had climbed to 2.2 per cent a year. Then, after World War II, a swift upsurge began. What happened?

While the birth rate has not changed much since the beginning of the century, the death rate has fallen sharply. Fewer Filipinos, especially young ones, have been dying of smallpox, malaria, and other preventable scourges. As a result, about 46 per cent of the citizens are under fifteen.

This pattern of population growth is a familiar one in many parts of the developing world of Asia, Africa, and Latin America. It is the pattern which is described by the oversimplified phrase "population explosion." Since no one seriously suggests increasing the death rate, it is the high birth rate that commands attention. Attitudes toward fertility depend on a number of factors. A society based on family equates numbers with prestige. An economy built on subsistence farming demands every pair of hands it can get. Where infant mortality remains stubbornly high, parents know they must build up insurance with large numbers of

*Almost half of the people in the Philippines are under
fifteen years of age. These children are from an island
in the Sulu Archipelago.*

children. Of this value system, a doctor with long experience
of working in Asia has said, "As long as a child remains an
economic asset instead of an economic liability, it will be
hard to convince a family that birth control is in its interest."

Where population presses on available resources, social
scientists see its growth as a serious threat to progress. But
they rightly offer no quick or easy solution. Filipinos, especially, are caught in a web of conflicting values, old and new.
In this dilemma, the factor of religion plays a surprisingly
minor role. The population "explosion" appears no less
explosive in Buddhist Ceylon or in Muslim Malaya than in
the Catholic Philippines.

For Filipinos the problem has irony as well as pathos.
Their population presses on available, not on potential, resources. The untapped, largely unexplored, resources of their
islands could support millions more people on an economic
level above any they have known. These talented people have
scarcely begun to be aware of the resources within themselves
and their land.

Life in the Past

The islands now known as the Philippines had been discovered, settled, cultivated, exploited, and fought over by Asians long before Europeans first sighted them. Some of the evidence of pre-European history survives in early written documents. But most of it had to be dug out of the soil of the islands themselves. In short, we owe to a small band of archeologists much of what is known about pre-European life and lore. The bulk of the treasure, scholars believe, still lies underground.

Among the early makers of Philippine history were highly literate peoples from the Asian mainland. Why did they apparently leave few written records of their presence on the islands? They *did* leave records in profusion. But Spanish missionaries destroyed most of them in the sixteenth century. Professor H. Otley Beyer, dean of Philippine archeologists, states that "the fanatic zeal of the Spaniards for the Christian faith and corresponding hatred for all other forms of belief led them to regard the native writings and art as works of the Devil—to be destroyed wherever found." One Spanish priest in southern Luzon boasted of having destroyed more than 300 scrolls written in native characters.

It was Professor Beyer's zeal which sparked an archeological treasure hunt. Digging began in earnest in 1926 in Rizal Province, near Manila. There diggers unearthed prehistoric stone implements believed to date from 250,000 years ago. The search continued with rich finds from historic times: gold ornaments, copper vessels, sacred images, drums and gongs, and Chinese porcelains of the Sung and Ming dynasties.

Three Civilizations

The archeological grist, added to a few surviving documents, suggests that three major civilizations largely shaped the history of the islands before the advent of Europeans. They were the Indian, the Arabic, and the Chinese civilizations.

Indian and Arabic influences reached the islands in somewhat diluted form, by way of the Southeast Asian mainland, and of Java, Sumatra, Borneo, and the other islands of the Indies. The Chinese infusion came straight and strong across the China Sea from its source on the continent.

Even before the birth of Christ, South Indian Buddhists began to discover the rich islands of the Indies and to convert their peoples. By the eighth century A.D., they had entrenched themselves sufficiently to found an "empire" of sorts in southern Sumatra. From its center at Sri-Vijaya, wandering colonists penetrated as far as the central Philippines, to which they gave their modern name, the "Visayas." The colonists made the islands of the Sulu Sea, to the south, a tributary by a treaty of marriage with a local chieftain. Thus began a 400-year trading boom for the islanders of the Sulu Sea, who learned to welcome ships from many parts of the empire, including Cambodia and what is now southeast China, as well as from the other islands of the Indies.

Toward the end of the thirteenth century, Sri-Vijaya fell before the onslaught of another Indian power. From neighboring Java, the Hindu Madjapahit Empire began to annex vassal states and spread its influence throughout the Indies. Now, for the first time, the island peoples were to feel an authentic imperial hand. With firearms from China, the Madjapahits began to impose colonial governors and collect taxes. The Philippines probably escaped with light controls, but there is evidence of Hindu influence as far north as central Luzon.

HINDUISM AND ISLAM

The Hindu culture left strong marks on Philippine language, laws, gods, and designs in dress, art, and armor. On Mindanao, diggers have found golden images of Vedic gods; on Cebu, bronze images; and on Panay, palm-leaf and bamboo manuscripts written in Indian characters. Tagalog, the Philippine national language, is heavily infiltrated with words borrowed from Sanskrit, the language of ancient India. On the basis of proven evidence, historians agree that of all the pre-European influences, it was the Hindu which most deeply penetrated the life and culture of the Philippines.

Indian culture, in turn, opened the door to Islam. It is ironic that the Spaniards took possession of a supposed

*Zamboanga, Mindanao. The Moro fisherman lives in this
kind of village, in a house built over the water on stilts.
His mosque is nearby.*

paradise only to find it occupied by the enemy they had
recently vanquished in Spain. In the Philippines, the Muslim
religion had had a 200-year head start over the Christian.
The first five Spanish friars who stepped ashore in 1565
found Islam already entrenched among the Malays of the
Sulu Sea and Mindanao. And they learned to their dismay
that the faith of the hated Moors had crept as far north as
central Luzon, the furthest expansion eastward ever achieved
by Islam. Recognizing their old antagonist the Moors in new
ethnic guise, the friars called these Malay converts "Moros."

Missionaries of the Prophet Mohammed first came to the
Sulu Islands around 1300 A.D. They were learned men.
They practiced advanced medicine, taught art, and preached
an exciting new faith. They came in peace, attached themselves to the courts of local chieftains, and ingratiated them-

A Moro wedding on the island of Mindanao.

selves by their wisdom. Not infrequently they married the chief's daughter. In this way one Abu Bakr became the first Sultan of Sulu. Where these missionaries originated is still not certain. Some scholars trace them to Malacca on the mainland; others to Java and Sumatra; still others to Islamic settlements in China. In any event, they stayed and made a lasting impact. The nature of their contribution has been well summarized by a Filipino scholar, Dr. Cesar Adib Majul:

". . . what gave the Moslems of Sulu their cohesion and sense of community was Islam. It was Islam that institutionalized their loyalties to their sultans, gave them a system of writing, sanctioned their attempts to resist alien rule, and gave a religious character to their patriotism. All of these constituted the ingredients for a form of prenationalism. It is, therefore, no accident that the places in the Philippines where the Spanish Sword and Cross met the most tenacious resistance were among those where Islam had already taken some root."

The blend of religious and political loyalty evoked by Islam has, as we shall see, managed to outlast and outwit almost every rival authority to this day.

THE ROLE OF THE CHINESE

China's interest in the Philippines could hardly have been more different. During almost eight pre-European centuries, the Chinese came to the islands not to conquer, colonize, or convert, but to trade. And they kept careful records of their business trips. In the ports of the Sulu Sea, where they found rich and profitable markets, they saw that "men and women cut their hair and wear a black turban and a piece of chintz with a minute pattern tied around them." The traders brought back stories of Sulu pearls measuring an inch in diameter, and of sea gypsies who cut off people's heads. The Chinese prudently traded from their ships, going ashore only occasionally and then well armed.

Between the tenth and fourteenth centuries A.D., trade rose in volume and flowed in both directions. To China went "yellow wax, cotton, pearls, tortoise-shell, medicinal betelnuts, and jute fibercloth." To the Philippines came Chinese "gold, iron, lead, glass beads, needles, cotton stuffs, red taffetas, ivory, silks, copper pots." The records claim that Sulu rajahs, with their wives, children, and headmen, came to the Chinese court bearing tribute in 1414 and 1420. By that time the Chinese merchants had gained courage to establish trading posts on Philippine coasts. At first they took native wives and raised their children as Malays. It was not until they came under the sheltering wing of Spanish colonial rule that the Chinese were encouraged to migrate in numbers and exploit the riches they had long coveted in the islands.

The First Europeans

European contacts with the Philippines began with hearsay. Marco Polo had heard of islands rich in spices, gold, and timber, east of the Asian mainland. Presumably Chinese traders had told him of the islands. He placed them in the "Sea of Chin," the China Sea. In his account of the "kingdoms and marvels of the East," he even numbered the islands at 7,459, a guess close to the actual number of the present-day Philippines. But he had no accurate notion of their location, and never visited them. In spite of Marco Polo, the very existence of the Philippines was virtually as unknown to Europe as the undreamed-of empires of Mexico and Peru.

It was the Portuguese, first among Europeans, who found and exploited a sea route to the riches of the East. After Vasco da Gama had sailed around the Cape of Good Hope to India, Portuguese seamen and warriors pushed eastward in search of the Spice Islands. One of these Portuguese, Francisco Serrano, helped in 1512 to found a trading post on the island of Ternate, in the Molucca group of what is now eastern Indonesia. In the same year Serrano landed on Mindanao, the largest island of the southern Philippines. He thus became the first European to set foot on Philippine soil.

Another of these bold and questing Portuguese was Ferdinand Magellan. He was a friend of Serrano's; both men had served in the East; and both had fought for Portugal against Arab traders and local rajahs. From correspondence with Serrano, and from a careful study of navigators' records and maps, Magellan concluded that he could reach the Spice Islands by sailing west. He failed to interest the King of Portugal in such a venture, since Portugal already had a virtual monopoly of the ship-borne trade in spices from the eastern islands. Accordingly, he took his plea and his plans to the King of Spain. It was thus that Magellan, a Portuguese, commanded a Spanish fleet of five ships which set out from near Seville in September 1519.

Along the South American coast, through the stormy strait that now bears his name, and across the vast Pacific, the five frail ships sailed their way into history. On March 16, 1521, they sighted the eastern shore of Samar in the Visayas. On the last day of the month Magellan landed on a small island south of Leyte, and took possession in the name of the King of Spain. He thus became, in European eyes at least, the discoverer of the Philippines.

Magellan did not live to complete his circuit around the world. While taking sides with one chieftain against another, Magellan was stabbed and hacked to death in a fight on the small island of Mactan, off Cebu. The chieftain who killed him, named Lapu Lapu, was destined to become, centuries later, a folk-hero of Philippine nationalism.

Only one of Magellan's five ships, with eighteen ragged, half-starved, and exhausted survivors, reached Seville in 1522. Its cargo of cloves, loaded at Tidore in the Moluccas on the homeward voyage, was worth more than the cost of the entire expedition. The survivors, luckily, included Antonio Pigafetta, a Venetian whose talent equalled the challenge of telling Magellan's story. Reading Pigafetta's journals, Europeans learned for the first time of the vast and unimagined extent of the Pacific and of the hazards of rounding South America through the southern strait. They learned, incidentally, of the existence of what would soon be called the Philippine Islands, in honor of Philip II of Spain.

Magellan and his men did not explore the interior of even those small islands they touched. They landed, raised the Cross, bartered with the islanders, and sailed away. In their brief stay they found nothing that would arouse the greed of their Spanish employers. The natives brought them oranges, coconuts, bananas, and rice—but no gold. For forty years after Magellan's visit, it was by no means sure that Spain would shape the Philippine future. The Spaniards were rich with plunder from the mines of the New World. Their power was stretched to the limit in organizing, extending, and defending their new empires in Mexico and Peru.

Spain did make three poorly planned, half-hearted efforts to reach the Philippines and the Spice Islands just to the southeast of them. All three met disaster, either through the hazards of the sea, or incompetent navigation, or the enmity of the Portuguese. Not until 1559 did King Philip II decide on a new attempt, backed by force, to conquer and Christianize the Philippines, to discover their products and resources, and to find a route back across the Pacific to New Spain and thence to the markets of Europe.

The new effort not only carried out the king's orders; it put the imprint of Spain on the Philippines for more than 300 years. That it succeeded so decisively was due in large part to its decisive leader, Miguel Lopez de Legaspi, a Basque who was a highly intelligent official of the capital of New Spain in Mexico City. He lacked experience as a navigator, but more than offset this lack by employing as his pilot an aging Augustinian friar, Andrés de Urdaneta, who had led an expedition to the Moluccas almost forty years before. Legaspi was a better leader of men than Columbus, less quarrelsome than Cortes, less greedy and brutal than Pizarro and the other freebooters who conquered Peru. He soon proved himself one of the ablest of all the Spanish proconsuls in the great age of colonial settlement.

Conquest and Conversion

The story of Legaspi's conquests can be briefly told. Sailing from the west coast of Mexico in November 1564 with five ships and 400 men, he reached Samar by February. Where local chieftains were unfriendly, he avoided them and sailed on to other islands. Where they were friendly, he made compacts with them and so gained allies for the future. He used force in order to plant his first settlement at Cebu, in the heart of the Visayas, but he quickly proved that he was a lenient ruler, concerned for the welfare of the people. In 1570, seeking greater safety from marauding Portuguese, he decided to move his capital to Manila. The future capital was then ruled by a Muslim rajah, Soliman, from the south. This time a bloody encounter, the "first Battle of Manila Bay," was needed before the Spaniards could subdue the town. Soliman was killed, to become, in the distant future, another hero of the independent Philippines. Legaspi laid out a new town on the ruins of the old.

From Manila, Legaspi sent out his lieutenants to explore and subdue the island of Luzon. One of them, Martin de Goiti, achieved an almost bloodless conquest of the fertile central Luzon plain. Legaspi's grandson, the brilliant Juan de Salcedo, achieved equal success around the coasts to the north and south. Everywhere the Spaniards' task was made easier by disunity among the local chieftains. The quarrelsome natives never combined their forces effectively enough to stop a few hundred armed and disciplined soldiers from Europe. By the time Legaspi died in 1572, Spanish rule had been accepted in the coastal and low-lying areas of Luzon and many of the Visayas. The chief areas not conquered were the mountainous interior of Luzon, not yet explored; Mindanao; and the other islands of the south. These were to remain unsubdued for three hundred years.

FOUNDATIONS OF UNITY

Considering the tiny forces at his disposal, Legaspi's was an achievement unsurpassed in the history of the Spanish Empire. Outwardly at least, he had united most of the scattered peoples of the Philippines and their local rulers under a single foreign power. No great army had to be sent from Spain to hold them. In this sense the conquests of Legaspi were an essential foundation, not only of Spain's 333-year rule, but also of Filipino nationalism.

It was not only the military conquest that made this unity possible. One of Spain's purposes in empire-building was to "Christianize" the native peoples. To "Christianize" meant, of course, to convert them to Roman Catholicism. The motive was not mere aggrandizement in territory and power. From the beginning to the end of Spain's centuries of empire, its kings honestly believed that Christianizing conferred the benefit and blessing of eternal life upon the subject

The might of Spain spoke through monuments like this— the Fort of Santiago in Manila. Built between 1584 and 1670, it was bombed by the Japanese in World War II.

peoples. Accordingly, Legaspi brought five friars with him to Cebu. They were the forerunners of hundreds.

The five learned the local dialect, and soon won astonishing successes in conversion. The Catholic ceremonies—the outdoor processions and the masses—were welcomed by a people who had always enjoyed ceremonials. The new religion encountered few obstacles among a spirit-ridden people. Sometimes those who resisted baptism fled to the hills, but they were in a minority. Only among the so-called Moros, strong in the faith of Islam, did the Catholic missionaries encounter continuous and violent hostility. The struggle against the Moros bedeviled the early Spanish leaders and priests, and baffled their successors for 300 years.

Except in Moro territory, Catholicism became a unifying influence at least as powerful as Spanish military rule. The Spanish Crown entrusted the friars with education and with what we would call social service, especially in the distant towns and villages. Five orders bore the heaviest part of the load: the Augustinians, Franciscans, Dominicans, Jesuits, and later, the Recollects. By shrewd persuasion used with a minimum of force, a few hundred friars from Spain were able to shape the religious and social life of most of the archipelago.

As the decades and centuries passed, the missionary orders became landowners. Some of the friars were corrupt and made themselves additionally disliked by refusing to admit Filipinos to the clergy. Yet in the first century of Spanish rule, individual friars showed much concern for the simple people in their charge. Sometimes they denounced the oppression and the occasional brutalities of the Spanish regime. As early as 1573 the Augustinian missionaries in Manila delivered a protest to the King of Spain, telling him that Spaniards were "held in ignominy in this country . . . because we maltreat our own friends and harass and trouble

*Catholicism dominates Filipino religious life. Here,
townspeople celebrate the festival of a patron saint by
carrying his image through the streets.*

them." Another who sided with the people was Bishop
Domingo de Salazar. He argued passionately against forced
labor and other exactions by the civil rulers and dared, in
1592, to take his protests personally to the great king in
Madrid.

CHRISTIAN ASIANS

Catholicism not only helped to unify the Philippines; it
also set the island people apart from the rest of Asia. Elsewhere in Asia, missionary Catholic orders won only limited
successes, converting a few millions in India, Ceylon, and

much later, Vietnam; nineteenth-century Protestants converted hundreds of thousands in Burma. Only in the Philippines was an Asian colony, a future independent nation, almost entirely Christianized. The conversion begun by Legaspi and the imposition of Spanish rule started the isolation of the Christian Philippines from Hindu, Buddhist, and Moslem Asia, an isolation which began to break only after independence in the mid-twentieth century. Communications and commercial policy added to this isolation and further cut off the Philippines from their Asian neighbors.

Early Spanish Legacies

Legaspi, the first conqueror, obeyed King Philip's orders to discover a homeward, eastward route across the Pacific. Because of the trade winds that blew from east to west in the latitude of the Philippines, sailing ships could not return by the same route from Mexico that brought them. Legaspi's navigator, Urdaneta, sought a homeward route by zigzagging northeastward through variable winds and frequent storms. When he reached the latitude of northern Japan, he picked up a steady west-to-east wind that carried him across the cold and islandless ocean almost to the coast of California. Then he steered south and southeast, well off the treacherous coast, until he reached the little port of Acapulco on the Pacific coast of Mexico.

This was to be the eastward route of Spanish ships until the age of steam. Whereas the voyage from Mexico to the Philippines usually took two or three months, with following winds and steady seas, the return voyage seldom took less than seven months. Such odysseys became tests of endurance as well as seamanship. The mortality rate aboard the cramped, high-sterned sailing ships often swept away more than half the passengers and crews. Those who disembarked at Acapulco were sometimes so weak and ill that they had to be carried from their ships. But the communications route had been established. Since the route through the Indies and around Africa was barred by Portuguese and other enemies, the Spaniards now had a way home free of interference except by the elements.

So it was that Spain's colony, Mexico, became the supplier of men and goods for the Philippines, and Mexican experience profoundly influenced the character of Spanish rule. With more than forty years' experience in Mexico, Spanish soldiers, administrators, lawyers, and priests had learned how to cow an alien people, how to Christianize them, how to extract labor and revenue from them. What was more natural, then, than for Spain to recruit its Philippine administrators from the veterans of Mexico? What could have been simpler than to apply the laws and institutions that had proved their effectiveness in Spanish America?

This is what the Mexican-trained Legaspi and his successors did. In organizing their new colony, it mattered little to them that the dry Mexican highlands were unlike the tropical Philippines in climate and in natural resources. In exploiting human resources, it mattered little that the warlike Aztecs differed in religion, temperament, and cultural background from the farmers and fishermen of the Far East. All were "Indians" to the early Spaniards, and all were handled in much the same way. If the modern Philippines appear to have many Latin-American rather than Asian characteristics, it is partly because Spain governed them for centuries as it governed its colonies in the New World.

From Mexico, for example, the Spaniards imported the system of a forced annual tribute. They fixed the prices of farm crops at so low a level that many a farmer had to abandon his fields and drift to the towns in search of work. Worse in its long-term effects on the Philippines was the same system of forced labor with which the Spaniards in Mexico had compelled the Aztecs to build churches, prisons, and public works. Throughout the Spanish period every male Filipino had to give forty days of labor each year to the government. Filipino nationalists of the twentieth century, seeking to account for the low productivity of Philippine farmers, still blame the Spanish system of tribute and forced labor for stifling initiative and for degrading rural labor.

Another Spanish experiment in the Philippines, copied from the colonies in the New World, was the creation of great feudal grants, or *encomiendas*. Legaspi rewarded his officers and others by letting them take tribute from the people on these huge tracts of land. The fortunate owner was required, on paper, to protect the people militarily, to school them, and to convert them; but, more important to the owner, he was entitled to take a portion of the people's crops and labor. In 1574 the king ordered the creation of private *encomiendas* stopped. They had become a threat, because the landholders could easily become petty tyrants, far from Manila and independent of government restraints. Instead, Spain divided the Philippines into provinces ruled by subordinates of the governor-general in Manila.

From then until the end of their 333-year rule in the Philippines, the Spaniards let nothing interfere with Manila's administrative supremacy. Legaspi founded a centralized government, necessarily so in a colony made up of thousands of islands and almost as many local chieftaincies. All lines of authority led to Manila. This centralization of government survived far longer than the imperial power of Spain. For when the Americans supplanted Spanish rulers, they, too, insisted on centralized rule. And when the Philippines finally won their freedom, their constitution-makers were careful for a variety of reasons (see pages 119–20) to keep the provinces firmly chained to Manila's central control.

Under the Spaniards, the governor-general (Legaspi was the first) was a potentate in the most literal sense. He commanded the armed forces; he made and unmade laws; and he appointed most officials—although even he had to depend on distant Madrid for funds. Alongside him rather than beneath him in the hierarchy sat the *Audiencia,* the high court, usually made up of professional judges trained in Mexico or in Old Spain. They not only heard and decided cases; they acted as referees in disputes between the governor-general and his subordinates, and they could appeal to the king himself against the governor-general.

Spain always set great store by legality and legalisms in governing its colonies. The lawyer held high prestige in the Philippines, as elsewhere in the Spanish colonial empire, an explanation, perhaps, of the multitudes of lawyers in the independent Philippines, and the high proportion of lawyers in government. The trouble in Spanish days, as now, was that enlightened laws were not well enforced. The so-called New Laws of 1542, launched in Mexico, were intended to protect the peasant against cruel or rapacious landlords. In large parts of the Spanish Philippines, and throughout the Spanish period, they remained laws on paper only, easily disregarded by Spanish administrators.

The China Trade

Not content with organizing the government of the new colony, Legaspi and his captains made determined efforts to search for gold, spices, and other valuable products for Spain. They found little gold and no spices of commercial importance except cinnamon and ginger. But shortly before his death in 1572, Legaspi made another commercial discovery that was to prove infinitely more valuable to Spain, and one that twisted and stunted the development of the Philippines for 300 years.

By accident, Legaspi discovered that Manila could become a way-station for the coveted silks, porcelains, and other goods of China. The accident was the sinking of a Chinese junk off the island of Mindoro. Its seamen were so grateful for their rescue by one of Legaspi's admirals, and for their good treatment in Manila, that they spread news about the Spanish masters of the Philippines on their return to China. The first result was the arrival the following year of ships from Canton and Amoy, laden with silks and porcelains, sugar and fruits. The traffic grew year by year. Manila paid for these cargoes in silver bullion from Mexico; the Chinese goods were loaded aboard slow-moving galleons, ships large and cumbersome for their time but strong enough to withstand the winds and waves of the North Pacific route back to Mexico.

For 250 years, once almost every year, a galleon from Manila made the perilous voyage to Mexico. Its goods, carried overland and shipped again to Spain, added to the overflowing riches of the Spanish Crown. The history of this trade, told in fascinating detail in William Lytle Schurz's *The Manila Galleon,* has little relevance here except for two points to be remembered. The first is that the galleon traffic made Manila, for most of the Spanish period, an entrepot port where traders and officials grew rich in the trade from China. The important event of each year was not anything that happened in the Philippines, but the arrival of the galleon from Mexico and its departure with its valuable cargo and passengers for home.

The second point, relevant to an understanding of the modern Philippines, is that the Spaniards saw no reason to develop the agricultural or mineral resources of the colony. They were convinced that the Philippines could offer them little compared to the profits to be won from the China trade. As a result, the rural Philippines were neglected until late in the Spanish period. Agriculture declined, commerce in foreign goods flourished. This was Legaspi's unhappiest legacy to the people whom his successors were to rule.

Another accident, comparable to the sinking of the junk off Mindoro, led to another far-reaching development that influences the Philippines to this day. This was an attack against the newly-founded Spanish settlement at Manila by a Chinese outlaw, Limahong, with a fleet of sixty-two ships and 3,000 men. Limahong almost succeeded in overwhelming the small garrison; Filipino allies helped the Spaniards to repel him. He was finally defeated the following year in the Gulf of Lingayen, northwest of Manila. His attack brought an official Chinese mission, searching for him. Satisfied that the Spaniards were disposing of him, the Chinese returned, bringing two Spanish officials and two missionaries to the court of the viceroy at Canton. The Spaniards failed, except for a brief period, to win direct access to a Chinese port. But the aftermath of these first official contacts was a sudden and continuous influx of Chinese into the Philippines, not only to trade but also to work as carpenters, craftsmen, and common laborers.

By 1590 more than 6,000 Chinese were living in Manila and its surroundings, most of them confined in a section just outside the city walls known as the Parian, across the Pasig River. The hard-working, adaptable Chinese quickly came to dominate the skilled trades on which the Spaniards in Manila depended. Although they were distrusted and feared, they proved themselves indispensable. From time to time they were discriminated against and persecuted. A revolt of the Chinese in 1603 spread terror through the Spanish community in Manila and led to the slaughter of an estimated 23,000 Chinese; another revolt in 1639 left only 7,000 Chinese alive; an order of expulsion in 1662 led to still another uprising. Yet the Chinese community revived, and immigration as well as intermarriage with the Filipinos continued. And in spite of recurrent hostility between the Spanish rulers and the Chinese in their midst, the treasure-laden junks continued to glide into Manila Bay, and the galleons continued to sail each year freighted with Chinese goods for Mexico and Europe. The basic pattern of most of three centuries of Spanish rule had been set in the first fifty years after Legaspi had raised the Cross and the flag of Castile in the Visayas.

The Spaniards used much of the existing structure of society as an underpinning of their own. When the system of private *encomiendas,* or land grants, was abolished, provincial government took its place. The provincial governments grouped the former *barangays,* or villages, into municipalities, but the *barangays* remained. Their chiefs or headmen, the *caciques,* were used to collect tribute, and functioned as servants of the Spanish regime without losing their prestige among their people. Slavery and the neighborhood wars of old were abolished, and church schools added a new dimension to rural life. But the all-important kinship system survived. Not to help kinfolk and friends remained a cardinal sin. Kinfolk in the Philippines meant the widest possible range of family connections: in-laws and adopted children as well as blood relatives. In spite of the tribute-money, forced labor, fixed prices, and other forms of Spanish control, the kinship system remained both an anchor and a drag on Philippine society, from pre-Spanish to post-Spanish days.

The Time of Troubles

After its bold beginnings, Spanish rule in the Philippines had to fight through many decades for its survival. Revolts flared repeatedly among the islands and each time had to be put down by the costly use of men and ships from Manila. Forced labor stirred special resentment. In 1622 and again in 1649–50, men of various Visayan islands killed Spanish officials and destroyed Spanish property to show their bitterness. More serious was a widespread revolt in central Luzon in 1660–61, again as a protest against forced labor. This time 40,000 rebels joined the anti-Spanish standard, and Manila had to use 6,000 troops to suppress them. In the eighteenth century, the revolts were aimed at the religious orders; the chief complaint was the taking of land that did not belong to them. One of these uprisings, in 1744, set up a separatist government on the island of Bohol. The separatists succeeded in ruling their island for more than eighty years. Not until 1827 was Manila able to reassert its control.

Along with these Filipino revolts, Manila had to fight repeated raids on the coasts by Moros, the Muslims of the southern islands. Like the Vikings in the Europe of a thousand years ago, the Moros would swoop without warning upon coastal towns, kill priests and officials, burn churches and houses, and load Christian captives as well as booty onto their ships. Again and again Manila sent expeditions southward to conquer the pirates in their lairs, but they always failed.

As if internal revolts and Moro attacks were not enough tribulation, the Spaniards had to combat recurrent naval attacks by the Portuguese, Dutch, and English. The first half of the seventeenth century was, in truth, a time of troubles for the Spanish rulers. The Dutch made four determined attempts to conquer Manila, once landing and holding part of the Bataan peninsula. These onslaughts failed, although Dutch and English at sea captured Spanish galleons from time to time. Not until the middle of the eighteenth century did anyone succeed in wresting Manila from the Spaniards. During the Seven Years' War in Europe, a British fleet captured the city and held it for two years. An energetic Spanish governor, Simón de Anda y Salazar, using Filipino as well as Spanish troops, kept the British cooped up in the Manila area. Under the Treaty of Paris in 1763, Spain regained Manila. Thus ended what was to be the only interlude of non-Spanish rule in 333 years.

The seventeenth century in the Philippines was a time of decline, and the eighteenth century one of stagnation. Spain had impoverished itself. Its Philippine possessions yielded nothing but deficits, in spite of the galleon trade. Spanish attempts to restrict trade with other countries, and to set up government monopolies, merely made the Philippines poorer; they did not make Spain richer. If one wonders why Spain did not develop the Philippines, did not start industries, did not exploit farms and mines with greater skill and drive, one explanation is surely the revolts and wars of the sixteen and seventeen hundreds. They strained the regime of the Spanish at home and drained its resources. They made it impossible for a weak and tired metropolitan power to do more than hold onto its Philippine outpost in the distant East.

First Flickers of Reform

Then, beginning in the eighteenth century, the shock of the English seizure of Manila, the currents of liberalism inspired by the French Revolution, and the subsequent revolts of the Spanish colonies in the New World, all jolted Madrid into a new awareness of the Philippines. Slowly, fitfully, the Filipino leaders and people awoke from the anesthetic of Spanish rule. From time to time Spain sent reformers to the East as governors. Always it eventually replaced them by narrow-minded bureaucrats, but the leaven of change had started to work. No amount of repression could stop it. At the beginning of the nineteenth century, the Philippines was not remotely ready to manage its own affairs. By the end of the century, it was ready in many ways for independence.

The changes made by the Spaniards were agricultural, commercial, political, social, and educational. The first breath of change was brought into the rural areas by a remarkable governor-general, José Basco y Vargas. He made the first intelligent efforts to reach the illiterate farmer and teach him scientific agriculture. He offered prizes to farmers and craftsmen for excellence. Under his regime, from 1778 to 1787, Spain formed a royal company to develop the cultivation of silk, cotton, sugar, and spices. All this was contrary to the old emphasis on the galleon trade and the corresponding neglect of Philippine resources. Basco made one backward step by forming government monopolies over tobacco, gunpowder, and wine. Nevertheless, he deserves to be remembered as one of the founders of the modern Philippines.

In commerce, the changes were more far-reaching and more lasting. Ships of other Western countries were allowed to use Philippine ports after the start of the nineteenth century. Foreign merchants, long excluded, set up offices and warehouses in Manila and other centers. Banks were opened, and ships arrived regularly from Spain itself rather than from Mexico. With the ending of the galleon trade in 1815, and the achievement of independence by Mexico a few years later, the Philippines' long dependence on Spain-in-Mexico disappeared. Ideas and men now came from Europe, along with thousands of Spanish settlers. The virtual seclusion of the Philippines had ended.

In political life, Spain at last made grudging concessions to the self-respect of its subjects. Filipino representatives—appointive, of course—took their places in the Spanish Cortes, or parliament, during three three-year periods, starting in 1810. Each time Spain revoked the privilege; Madrid obviously followed no consistent or well thought-out policy toward its subject people in the Orient. But the memory of representation in the Cortes remained alive among educated Filipinos and made them yearn for greater political participation.

In social life, one innovation, barely noticed at the time, left a lasting mark on the Philippines. This was the bestowal of Spanish surnames on baptized children. Until 1849 a Filipino child received a Spanish Christian name at baptism, but no surname. This confused and hampered the friars who were responsible, under the Spanish system, for schooling as well as for the spiritual welfare of the Filipinos. From a long list of Spanish family names, parents were asked to choose one for their newly baptized child. These were no made-up names like those provided for the Jews of Europe·in the time of Napoleon I. Many of them were proud Castilian names borne by Spanish families for many centuries.

Names like García, López, and Rodriguez soon became common in the Philippines. An educated Filipino might not have a drop of Spanish blood, but if he went to Spain, as many did in the nineteenth century, his name gave him a sense of equality with the most patrician Spaniard. However, the Spanish names deceived other Asians into thinking that all Filipinos were *mestizos,* of mixed Spanish-Filipino blood, and not Asian at all. The new names, therefore, became both an asset and a handicap to the Philippine people. They brought self-respect along with a sense of alienation not only from the rest of Asia but from the Philippines' own non-

Spanish past. To read the roll of the Philippine Senate, for example, or the graduating class at a university, is to imagine that all the members must be Spanish or part-Spanish in their ancestry. In many instances they are, but often they are pure Filipino or mixed Filipino-Chinese.

In still another field, education, the nineteenth-century Spaniards began making up for ancient neglect. Vocational schooling made its long-delayed appearance, starting with a nautical college in 1820 to train seamen. The Spanish authorities also recognized, at long last, that they had left the friars in charge of education for far too long. A decree of 1863, imperfectly carried out, provided for a publicly supported primary school in each town, one for boys and one for girls. With the slow growth of literacy, the government permitted the publishing of newspapers. These were feeble plants. Each lived only a few years, but the early journals were forerunners of the vigorous, uninhibited Philippine press of the present day. The old, established Spanish universities, notably Santo Tomas in Manila, now found literate youngsters clamoring for admission. After 1865 Santo Tomas granted an average of fifty-eight degrees a year, four times the number at the start of the century.

LIMITATIONS OF THE REFORM

The trouble with most of these changes—agricultural, political, educational, social—was that they went only skin-deep. They did not penetrate to the defects in Spanish rule. Forced labor remained a cancer in Philippine life. Justice was available to the rich, at a price, but beyond the reach of the illiterate poor. Censorship and bureaucracy stifled free expression in newspapers, books, and public meetings. The injustices of land tenure grew worse in the nineteenth century. Due to absentee ownership, only 5 per cent of the cultivable land was being farmed. And by 1898, the last year of Spanish rule, only about 200,000 children were attending elementary schools, religious and secular, in a population of seven million. This was hardly mass education, if, indeed, mass education had been the intent of the education decree of 1863.

But herein, perhaps, lay part of the key to the superficial quality of Spanish reform and its subsequent failure. The education decree, at least, was inspired in large part by motives other than a desire for real change. Like similar laws made for the mother country itself, it had insufficient will (and money) behind it. The educational reform was primarily planned as a snub to the Church and a concession to a new Filipino anticlericalism. As in Spain, the motives were mainly defensive—an attempt to placate internal discontent. In Spain during the middle of the nineteenth century, there was not only increasing hatred of the Church but a restive labor force as well. To please its anticlerical public and at the same time to replenish its chronically meager funds, in the 1850's the Spanish government took Church property and sold it. A new education law in 1857 also delighted the anticlericals and annoyed the Church: it called for an increase in the number of public primary schools and for an end to theology courses in the secular universities.

In the Philippines, a fierce anticlericalism had grown up in response to the behavior of the Spanish clergy. The Spanish friars, who had begun their work in rural areas as benevolent teachers, had too often become greedy, corrupt, and resistant to change. The missionary orders had become a state within a state, and neither the archbishops nor the civilian-military government in Manila seemed able to control them. In the mid-nineteenth century, Filipinos developed two main grievances against the missionary orders. First, the friars resisted pleas to admit more Filipinos to the clergy as parish priests. Second, the missionary orders owned 400,000 acres of good farm land, much of which the farmers felt was theirs by law and right.

THE ROAD TO REVOLT

The education reform not only failed to improve education, but it failed to remove the causes of anticlericalism as well. In the absence of effective government action, Filipinos themselves, and particularly Filipino priests, organized for change. One of these was Father José Burgos, an outstanding graduate of Santo Tomas University. Burgos and other Filipino priests allied themselves with well-to-do laymen to promote the so-called Filipinization of the clergy.

A short-lived liberal revolt in Spain in 1868 brought a ray of hope. A reformist governor, Carlos Maria de la Torre, arrived from Madrid and promptly sought to placate the Filipinos. He abolished censorship and pardoned rebels who were being hunted as outlaws. In a bold act that foreshadowed President Magsaysay's offer to the Huk rebels in the 1950's, de la Torre invited the former rebels to form a police force. De la Torre, like Governor Basco of the previous century, won an honored place for himself in Philippine history.

But Spain neither honored him nor carried out his reforms. A reactionary government replaced him with a narrow and arrogant governor. A minor mutiny in the military arsenal at Cavite, at the entrance to Manila Bay, gave the new governor a chance to strike at all those who had championed the cause of reform. Father Burgos, with two other Filipino priests, Mariano Gómez and Jacinto Zamora, were sentenced to death, although they had had no hand in the Cavite uprising.

One by one the priests had the iron collar fastened around their necks. All were slowly strangled by the *garrotte,* the agonizing Spanish form of execution of those days. Thus, three centuries after Legaspi's landing in Manila, the Philippines acquired their first national martyrs.

Young men of talent, finding the atmosphere of the Philippines stifling, became expatriates in Spain, studying, writing, and propagandizing for a new deal for the Filipinos. Other young men, remaining in the islands, turned to secret plotting. Both groups were finding the road to revolution. It was a road paved with Spanish blunders. Soon it would be drenched with Filipino and foreign blood.

The Emergence of
the Modern Philippines

Like the French and Russian revolutions, the Philippine struggle for independence began as a reform movement. Its first leaders were men of nonviolence. Most of them were sons of well-to-do families, of the tiny elite which had the money to send its youths abroad for higher learning.

In the beginning their goals did not include independence. What they wanted, rather, was a new status for the Philippines: that of a province, an integral part of Spain. With such a status, they thought, the Philippines would send its delegates to the Spanish parliament. The reformers also talked and wrote against social evils in the Philippines: the domination of the clergy by Spaniards, the suppression of free discussion and inquiry, the virtual exclusion of the poor from justice and fair dealing.

79

In the Spanish Philippines such protest—any protest—was akin to treason. The young reformers, not wishing to court jails at home, did most of their organizing and propagandizing in the freer air of Europe: in Paris, London, and before long, in Madrid itself.

In Europe they learned new ideas and ideals that were stirring students and workers in almost every country, even in reactionary Spain. They discovered that social justice, compulsory schooling, and public welfare were already far advanced. By the early 1890's, socialism was already a political force in European capitals and factory towns. Compulsory secular schooling was already in effect in France, Switzerland, Great Britain, and parts of Germany. Many governments had long recognized that they, rather than a church, were responsible for the health and welfare of their citizens.

Living and studying in this heady atmosphere, the young Filipinos gained a new perspective on their own repressed islands. In addition, they learned the techniques of propaganda and protest. Every European capital sheltered overt or underground organizations bent on changing the status quo, by agitation if not by force. Meeting some of their leaders and carefully reading their publications, the Filipinos set out to master their techniques and to use them. In Madrid their chief instruments were a new Spanish-Filipino association and its journal, called *La Solidaridad* (*Solidarity*). A contributor to this journal was José Rizal, who was to become his nation's hero.

José Rizal

Born in 1861 into a family of many ethnic strains, including Spanish and Chinese, Rizal was a young man of extraordinary gifts. He not only practiced as an eye doctor, but was also a linguist, a poet, and an accomplished student of medicine, philosophy, and law. Above all, Rizal was a propagandist. He was only twenty-six when, brooding about the sorrows of his native Philippines, he wrote his famous first novel, *Noli Me Tangere.* (The literal translation is *Don't Touch Me,* but English translations have been entitled, more expressively, *The Lost Eden* and *The Social Cancer.*) In the book, Rizal exposed many social cancers: the greed of Spanish friars, the arrogance of Spanish governors, the submissiveness of his own people after almost 350 years of Spanish rule. As one of his characters said, "The people do not complain because they have no voice; they do not move because they are in a stupor."

Rizal's first novel has often been called the *Uncle Tom's Cabin* of the Philippines. This is not quite accurate, for *Uncle Tom* aroused a largely literate North in the United States, whereas the Philippines had only a small elite who could read. Nevertheless, *Noli Me Tangere* and a second novel, *El Filibusterismo* (*The Subversives*), acted as an electric shock among educated Filipinos in Europe and at home. Copies smuggled into the Philippines promptly marked their author as a subversive.

Rizal returned to the Philippines in 1892 to help form La Liga Filipina ("Filipino League"), an association which pressed for educational, economic, and social changes. The colonial government answered by deporting him to Dapitan, a small town on the coast of far-off Mindanao. There he taught school and bided his time. When Cuba revolted against Spain in 1895, Rizal set off as a volunteer doctor to work among the Spanish troops. But the suspicious Spanish government pulled him off a ship in the Mediterranean, arrested him, and tried him for treason.

José Rizal, the Philippines' national hero, when he was a student. Rizal wrote his first propagandist novel when he was only twenty-six.

The verdict was foreordained. On the Luneta, the grassy space that looks out toward red sunsets on Manila Bay, Rizal met his death. The Spaniards denied him even the last proud gesture of facing his firing squad. He left a farewell poem, an ode to his country, written the night before he was executed.

That such a man should have become the national martyr was of lasting value to the Philippines. Rizal lived too short a time to prove his political capacity, or even his skill as a revolutionary leader. Yet he bequeathed to his people a civilian hero in an intellectual rather than a military mold, a father-figure in the gentle manner of Lincoln and Gandhi. In the decades that followed the fatal volley on the Luneta, Filipinos experienced revolution, war, and recurrent violence. But their ideal was never the man on horseback; it remained, and remains to this day, the poet-novelist-lawyer-doctor who gave his life in his nation's cause.

Unlike Rizal in background, temperament, aims, and tactics were the men who became revolutionary leaders after his death. These were the organizers of a secret society, the Katipunan. (Its full name, translated from Tagalog, was "Highest and Most Venerable Association of the Sons of the Nation.") They formed it when Rizal was deported to Mindanao in 1892. The Katipunan plotters were, for the most part, poor and frustrated men. Their goal was more than reform; it was social revolution, as well as total separation from Spain. Using a secret code and passwords, printing a secret newspaper, organizing provincial and local councils without the Spaniards' knowledge, they caused the Katipunan movement to spread with the speed of a Philippine typhoon.

For four years the Spanish authorities heard only vague rumors of its existence. So well kept was the secret that the

*On the left is Apolinario Mabini, the intellectual
leader of the Philippine War of Independence, and
on the right, General Emilio Aguinaldo, the
military leader of the struggle.*

Katipunan grew to have more than 100,000 members,
mostly in Luzon, before the Spaniards knew of it. Finally, in
August 1896, an employe of a printing plant told a priest
about the movement and its plans for a revolt, and the priest
told the government. This struck the spark: the war for Philippine independence had begun.

The War for Independence

THE FIRST STAGE

The revolutionary leaders fled to the hills. With their movement unmasked, their plans disclosed, they lost no time in calling for an uprising. Spanish garrisons were attacked, and detachments were ambushed in widely scattered parts of Luzon, and even in the Visayas. Spain fought back not only with bullets and bayonets, but with terror. Mass arrests filled the jails. Suspicion and punishment were meted out to anyone who might sympathize with the revolt, whether or not he belonged to the Katipunan conspiracy. Rizal was only one of hundreds of victims. It was the discovery of the secret society which provoked his trial and execution.

As the rebels gained in strength and daring, the war grew savage on both sides. The rebels reserved their choicest tortures for the hated Roman Catholic friars. The Spaniards spread their brutalities impartially. Late in 1897 rebels and Spaniards alike had wearied of the bloodletting. Both sides agreed to a truce, under which Spain promised reforms and a payment of $850,000 to the insurgent leaders and to the families of their fighting men. A peace agreement was signed, and an uneasy lull settled over the islands.

By this time leadership of the revolution had passed to new hands. Rizal, who never wanted full independence, was dead; the once-secret Katipunan had been abolished and merged with other groups wanting freedom from Spain. Its founder, Andrés Bonifacio, a rabble-rouser rather than a leader, wrangled with his new colleagues and before long was arrested and shot by the rebels themselves.

By 1897 the new leader was a 28-year-old soldier, Emilio Aguinaldo, a brave but intellectually narrow combatant against Spain. It was Aguinaldo's command of guerrilla tactics, his burning hatred of the Spanish regime, his capacity for rousing the villagers and workers, that fanned the flames of revolt and kept them blazing. Aguinaldo was no thinker and did not pretend to be. The brain-power behind the revolution now came from his chief counselor, Apolinario Mabini. A law graduate of Santo Tomas University, Mabini had been stricken with paralysis in 1895, and could help Aguinaldo only from a cripple's chair. Of all the early heroes of Filipino nationalism, none could compare in effectiveness with Aguinaldo and Mabini.

Aguinaldo and thirty-four other rebel leaders sailed for temporary exile in Hong Kong on December 30, 1897, just a year after Rizal had been shot. Armed with the first $200,000 installment of the Spanish payment, they resumed plotting, propagandizing, and shopping for weapons. They did not have to wait long before a dramatic and unexpected event revived the revolution and ended Spanish rule. This, of course, was the Spanish-American War of 1898, fought ostensibly to set Cuba free.

UNITED STATES INVOLVEMENT

Soon after dawn on May 1, 1898, Commodore of the United States Navy George Dewey ordered: "You may fire when you are ready, Gridley." By noon the entire Spanish fleet was a heap of junk on the bottom or in the shallows of Manila Bay. On May 20, 1898, Emilio Aguinaldo again set foot on Philippine soil, brought back on an American revenue cutter with Dewey's permission.

The two events were to have lasting effects on the Philippines. The first signaled the intrusion of American power and influence into the lives of the Filipinos. The second announced that Philippine nationalism had come to stay.

If history were logical, the two movements would have become allies. Aguinaldo himself thought for a time that the Americans would help him and recognize him as leader of the independent Philippines. Had not the United States been saying for more than a century that it was not, and would not become, a colonial power? When Aguinaldo had visited Singapore in April, the American consul there had taken it upon himself to repeat the same anti-colonial sentiments. In Hong Kong, just after the Battle of Manila Bay, the American consul had regarded Aguinaldo as a valuable helper against Spain and had even agreed to sell him arms.

Dewey himself was more guarded. He did give Aguinaldo encouragement. In a conference aboard his flagship, Dewey told Aguinaldo he could take whatever he wanted of arms, ammunition, and stores from the captured Spanish arsenal at Cavite. To the end of his days—he lived to be ninety-four— Aguinaldo insisted that Dewey had promised him more. But no written promise from Dewey ever came to light, and the Commodore, soon to become Admiral, steadfastly denied having made one, written or oral. At the time of the Battle of Manila Bay and for long months after, the United States simply did not know what to do with or about the Philippines. The McKinley Administration, not yet having a policy, temporized. It would neither recognize Aguinaldo as an ally nor, for the moment, oppose him.

Aguinaldo did not let uncertainty deter him. He was primarily a man of action, and he proceeded to act, militarily and politically. With the arms from Cavite and with others captured from the Spaniards, he soon had 30,000 men under his command. They were beginning to be a disciplined force, as victories over Spanish garrisons soon proved.

The city of Manila remained in Spanish hands while Dewey, on his flagship in the bay, awaited infantry from home. Aguinaldo proceeded to encircle Manila on land. By July the city was under siege. The first American troops took up beachhead positions by pushing Aguinaldo's forces, bloodlessly but firmly, aside. On August 13, 1898, after what was little more than a sham battle to preserve Spanish honor, the city surrendered. The Spanish flag was hauled down after 333 years of colonial rule. What took its place was not the banner of Philippine nationalism, but the Stars and Stripes. The rebels had been warned not to enter their capital city without American permission; otherwise, American troops would fire on them.

The First Republic

Meanwhile, as tension built up between Americans and insurgents, Aguinaldo had hurried to build a new government. On June 12, 1898, he proclaimed the independence of the Philippines, and promptly asked for the formal recognition of foreign powers. The United States chose not to notice, not to become involved, and not to take the new regime seriously. (Sixty-two years later, the date of Aguinaldo's proclamation, June 12, became the official Independence Day of the Republic of the Philippines.)

In September, Aguinaldo convened a congress, a constituent assembly, for the chief purpose of writing a constitution. The meeting-place was the market town of Malolos, some forty miles northeast of Manila. About a hundred delegates from most of Luzon, and from many of the outer islands, assembled for their task in the ancient stone church. Whereas Aguinaldo and most of the leaders of the new government came from the poor and the dispossessed, the delegates included well-to-do intellectuals and members of old *cacique* families. The delegates debated more than two months.

On November 29, 1898, they adopted a document of high quality. The Malolos Constitution, as it is called, was not especially novel in its machinery of government. It set up three separate branches—legislative, executive, and judicial— as in the United States, but gave the legislature proponderant power. There was to be a one-chamber assembly which would elect the national president. The cabinet of seven men would be responsible not to the president but to the assembly, and its members would have seats on the floor. A permanent assembly commission would insure continuance of legislative supremacy while the assembly was not in session.

The Filipinos, in other words, were eclectic and selective, as they have always been. (See pp. 33–37.) As government-builders, they took some ideas from the American presidential system and some from the European parliamentary systems.

More remarkable, in the Philippine setting of 1898, were two aspects of the Malolos charter. The first was its overtone of social revolution: its provisions for separating church and state, nationalizing church lands and buildings, schooling all children free of charge, electing provincial and municipal assemblies. The second was a sweeping bill of rights, unprecedented in Asia, more specific and detailed than that in the Constitution of the United States. With three centuries of rigid Spanish rule behind them, the drafters boldly took safeguards from Magna Carta and from Anglo-American experience, and decreed them as applicable to every Filipino. Concern for individual liberty thus leaped from Britain and the United States halfway around the globe.

Were the Filipinos of 1898 entitled to independence? Undeniably, they were. Few Americans, even at that zenith of colonialism, dared to argue that the Filipinos had no abstract right to manage their own affairs. Were they ready for independence? Obviously Aguinaldo and his colleagues thought they were ready. The Filipinos had produced intelligent leaders, a devoted army, an enlightened constitution, and a discernible national spirit.

By Western standards, however, the 7 million Filipinos of 1898 were far from ready. They were overwhelmingly illiterate and inexperienced in self-government except at the village level. They had no civil service of their own, no leaders who had ever managed official departments, no tradition of responsible politics, virtually no industries to supplement their simple agriculture, and, what was most important in the context of 1898, no prospect of being able to defend their islands against acquisitive foreign powers, of which the United States was not the only one.

Several motives caused the United States to take and keep the Philippines. One, of course, was hunger for new markets as well as raw materials. Another was the missionary urge among American Protestants, some of whom saw a golden opportunity of replacing the Roman Catholic friars of Spain. Still another, personified by Theodore Roosevelt and Senator Albert J. Beveridge, was sheer expansionism: the joy of flexing American muscles, of coloring another part of the world map red, white, and blue. But none of these motives was as compelling as Washington's fear that some other power would seize the Philippines if the United States did not.

This fear concerned a much wider area than the Philippines. China in 1898 appeared to be in a state of dissolution, and several European powers were jockeying for positions from which to attack the carcass. Germany, Russia, France, and Britain already held concessions on the China coast. To some uneasy American officials, and to high officers of the Army and Navy, it looked as if the United States might be shut out of trade with China by the new European seizures of Chinese ports. Germany gave substance to these American misgivings, not only by actively seeking territory in China but also by unfriendly gestures in the Philippines. In Manila Bay shortly after Dewey's victory, the Germans kept watch over German "interests" with a fleet that was stronger than that of the United States. The German commander treated Dewey's blockade with studied disrespect.

Aware of this background, President McKinley moved step by step in the last half of 1898 to keep the Philippines under American control. At first, he wanted only a naval base in the Philippines. His instructions to the American peace commission in September went further and called for American sovereignty over the entire island of Luzon. By October, the President ordered the American negotiators to demand cession of the whole archipelago.

American Rule

Expressions of American moral purpose, of obligation to the long-oppressed Filipinos, even of a destiny imposed by God—all these could not conceal the underlying motive. In taking the Philippines, the McKinley Administration was no whit more moral than the British and French had been in their colonial acquisitions of the previous decade. The Americans, like the British in northern Burma and the French in western Indochina, grabbed territories to keep others from grabbing. In one sense, however, McKinley's decision was actually less moral than those of the European colony-builders. For the United States, alone among the major nations, had loudly disavowed any intention to rule foreign peoples. In the Treaty of Paris which formally ended the "splendid little war" with Spain, the United States tried to make its action look more respectable. It agreed to pay Spain $20 million for the Philippines, but America's "image," as it would be called today, remained smudged. If President McKinley had been less careful to wrap his actions in moral words, he might have boasted, as Theodore Roosevelt did about the Panama Canal Zone a few years later, "I took the Philippines."

Speaking long afterward at a meeting with the General Missionary Committee of the Methodist Episcopal Church, McKinley confessed that he had "walked the floor of the White House night after night" and "prayed Almighty God for light and guidance more than one night." "Late one night," he said,

> It came to me this way—I don't know how it was but it came: (1) that we could not give them [the Philippines] back to Spain—that it would be cowardly and dishonorable; (2) that we could not turn them over to France or Germany —our commercial rivals in the Orient—that would be bad business and discreditable; (3) that we could not leave them to themselves—they were unfit for self-government—and they would soon have anarchy and misrule over there worse than Spain's; and (4) that there was nothing left for us to do but to take them all, and to educate the Filipinos, and uplift and civilize and Christianize them, and by God's grace to do the very best we could by them, as our fellowmen for whom Christ died, and then I went to bed, and went to sleep and slept soundly . . .

The President believed every word of this. He even felt the need to "Christianize" a people already overwhelmingly Roman Catholic. More remarkable, as the record will show, he and his Administration ultimately did "do the very best we could by them."

The decision to keep the Philippines led to one of the bitterest debates of American political history. A large, influential, and vocal minority opposed it, in Congress and in the nation. So close was the Senate vote on the peace treaty itself, taken on February 6, 1899, that a switch of two votes would have been enough to reject it.

What swung the doubting Senators may well have been a fusillade two days earlier on the other side of the world. For on the night of February 4, two American sentries shot at Filipino troops who had entered the American lines. The Filipinos returned the fire. The shooting spread. The United States now had a nasty war on its hands, a war against Filipinos whom it wanted to "uplift and civilize," a war that would cost far more in men and money than America's "splendid little war" against Spain.

In American histories it is usually called "the Philippine insurrection." Filipinos call it, with more truth, a renewal of the War for Philippine Independence.

PACIFICATION

To Aguinaldo and his fellow fighters, the American decision dealt a double blow. First, it hurt to realize that the Filipinos were being forced to exchange Spain's rule for that of another Western power. Second, it hurt because the new enemy soon eroded some of Aguinaldo's most valuable support. Many rich and educated Filipinos, including some who had drafted the Malolos Constitution, drifted away from Aguinaldo and made their peace. Every American offer of amnesty, every American protestation of good will, attracted more of these essentially conservative men away from Aguinaldo's cause. Some of them hurried to put themselves at the service of the invaders. They thought, correctly, that their property would be safer and their talents put to better use if they cooperated with the United States.

Aguinaldo, for his part, was a born fighter. So was Mabini, who could fight only with his intellect and not with his paralyzed body. What they lost by the desertion of the rich and well-born they more than made up in growing support in the rural *barrios*. Early in 1899, the Americans sent troops into central Luzon; they captured and burned Malolos, the rebel capital, and pushed on. But Aguinaldo's men simply slipped away into the hills. Villagers supplied them with food, and hid the Filipino troops when necessary. When the inevitable drenching rains came, the Americans found that victory, like the Filipinos, had eluded them.

Repeated reinforcements from home brought the American army in the Philippines to a strength of 74,000 officers and men. This was more than the British had needed in 1885–87 to conquer and pacify Burma. The American commanders at last discovered what they had refused to believe or tell Washington in 1898 and 1899: that Aguinaldo had popular support. The fight, then, was not just a police action against a rebellious minority; it had to be an all-out war.

At the height of the struggle the Americans fought it in all-out fashion, burning villages and taking hostages. They were even accused of applying the so-called "water cure," forcing water into prisoners in an effort to extort information about guerrillas. The Secretary of War, Elihu Root, conceded in 1902 that some individuals in the American forces had been "unnecessarily and unjustifiaby cruel." But, he said, such acts had violated strict orders—and the United States had been fighting enemies "who totally disregarded the laws of civilized warfare and who were guilty of the most atrocious treachery and inhuman cruelty."

All-out methods succeeded. The end came through a ruse. Brigadier General Frederick Funston and three other American officers, using a band of Filipino turncoats, pretended to be their prisoners. In this disguise they trekked inland to Aguinaldo's hideaway in northeastern Luzon. There they surprised and captured him—and the long, bloody "insurrection" was virtually over. Aguinaldo sullenly took the oath of allegiance to the United States. Mabini, still unyielding in his hard and bitter mind, was deported to Guam; he was repatriated in time to die on home soil in 1903.

By July 4, 1901, civilian governors had replaced soldier-rulers everywhere except in southern Mindanao and the Sulu islands. In these outposts of habitual rebellion against authority, the Moros in large numbers refused to be reconciled

Scenes from the United States pacification of the Philippines in 1899. Above, American troops from a Minnesota regiment in their trenches. Below, Filipinos who paid the price of rebellion.

to American rule. Not until 1915 did a civilian governor take charge of the Muslim islands. Nevertheless, the "insurrection" was formally ended on July 4, 1902, when the United States proclaimed peace and amnesty. It had been a hard and bitter war, far harder than the expansionists of 1898 had foreseen.

PREPARATION FOR HOME RULE

Essentially, the period of American sovereignty over the Philippines was one of preparation. It prepared the Filipinos for what was first called home rule, then self-government, then total independence. The preparation began even while Americans were fighting Aguinaldo's army, and even before the Administration in Washington knew precisely what it was preparing the Filipinos for. Where American garrisons were installed—there were 639 of them in towns and villages in 1901—American soldiers were taken off their guard duties to teach children and to restore public services.

Early in 1899, with the Filipino-American war in full swing, President McKinley sent out a commission headed by President Jacob Gould Schurman of Cornell University. Its assignment was to investigate conditions and recommend a future course. The commission found the Filipinos "totally unprepared for independence." It did, however, recommend a speedy start of civil government wherever possible. And it assured the Filipinos of President McKinley's purpose "to grant as large a measure of home rule and as ample liberties as were consistent with the ends of government . . ."

This, of course, was too vague to be a binding pledge to the Filipinos or a guide to the Americans who were starting to rule them. Such a pledge and guide came in a set of instructions from President McKinley to the Second Philippine Commission, headed in 1901 by William Howard Taft.

Drafted by Elihu Root, the Secretary of War, with additions and changes by Taft himself, the instructions were a virtual charter of preparation for self-government.

The document set out priorities for the American authorities. The first was to set up local governments, in the cities and the countryside, with the greatest possible measure of Filipino self-rule. The second was to form county or provincial governments.

"In all cases," the commission was told, "the municipal officers who administer the local affairs of the people are to be selected by the people . . . Wherever officers of more extended jurisdictions are to be selected in any way, natives of the Islands are to be preferred . . ."

The instructions called for individual liberty, for the "real, entire and absolute" separation of church and state, for free primary education, and for the use of English in place of Spanish as a common medium throughout the multilingual islands. But it was the President's general injunctions rather than the specific ones which set the tone of American rule in the Philippines for decades:

> . . . the commission should bear in mind that the government which they are establishing is designed, not for our satisfaction or for the expression of our theoretical views, but for the happiness, peace and prosperity of the people of the Philippine Islands, and the measures adopted should be made to conform to their customs, their habits, and even their prejudices . . .

Only when those customs clashed with "certain great principles of government" could Americans override them. Slavery, for example, was forbidden in 1903 in the Moro (Muslim) territories formerly ruled by the Sultan of Sulu in the southern islands. In general, however, American administrators were told to hold the reins lightly:

Upon all officers and employees of the United States, both civil and military, should be impressed a sense of the duty to observe not merely the material but the personal and social rights of the people of the islands, and to treat them with the same courtesy and respect for their personal dignity which the people of the United States are accustomed to require from each other.

In Filipino experience it was nothing new for a colonial master to profess noble motives. The Spanish Crown had done so from the earliest days, only to have its precepts flouted by civil and military officials in the colony. Americans, too, permitted lapses from their high standards. Yet, in general, American civilian administrators did live up to the McKinley-Taft-Root instructions. By appointing Filipinos to high positions, by recognizing the "personal dignity" of Filipino civilians, by showing a concern for the health and welfare of the people, the Americans soon wiped out most of the bitterness of the "insurrection," the Filipinos' Lost Cause.

COLONIAL BORROWINGS

One must not imagine that everything the Americans did in their first decade bore a peculiarly American stamp. On the contrary, the possession of a colony was wholly outside American experience, and was in itself an imitation of European practice. From the Spaniards the Americans virtually copied the office of governor-general; the genial Taft held powers as sweeping as those of an autocratic Spanish viceroy. From the Dutch in the nearby East Indies, and from other colonial powers, the Americans copied the economic philosophy of regarding their colony primarily as a source of raw materials. (See pages 144–48.)

From British imperial practice, the Americans borrowed more. The emphasis on law and order, and on impartial and incorruptible justice; the prompt creation of an insular police force known as the Philippine Constabulary; the building of roads and the improvement of other communications; the enforcement of strict honesty among American officials and the attempt to inculcate it among their Filipino subordinates —all these, and many others, were British priorities which the Americans adopted in their first Oriental possession.

British and Spanish, too, was the preference of the American regime for keeping the social structure intact and for governing with the help of rich and conservative local leaders. (See pages 44 and 70.) It was these part-Spanish descendants of local chieftains to whom the Americans turned when they needed Filipinos for important governmental posts.

AMERICAN FEATURES

Yet the new regime was also unmistakably American. What made it so was not so much the informality of the civilian officials, their easy familiarity with the Filipinos, their lack of pomp and stiffness. What mattered was a set of basic assumptions which the Americans brought to the Islands.

One of these was the assumption that only an educated people could ever manage its own affairs. The American passion for free, compulsory, and secular primary schooling was unique in the long history of Western colonialism. The effects on the future republic were deep and lasting. (See pages 37, 176, and 179.)

A second American assumption was the need for complete separation of church and state. The Roman Catholic Church could continue its religious work, but only on the same basis as in the United States. The Americans, moreover, were determined to remove the bitterest grievance left from Spanish rule: the ownership of 400,000 acres of productive Philippine farmland by Roman Catholic orders. Governor Taft, going to Rome in 1903, persuaded the Vatican to sell most of these lands to the Philippine Commission for $7,543,000. The Commission, in turn, sold them in small parcels to Filipinos. (See page 161.) In buying and re-selling the church lands, the American regime won new good will among the Philippine people.

A third American assumption was that the Filipinos must "learn by doing," and learn quickly, in managing their own political affairs. It was not enough for them to dabble their toes in political waters. They must be allowed and encour-aged to swim. They must choose their leaders, staff their government, write and pass their laws, raise their own taxes, and thus learn responsibility without delay.

Of all the American innovations in the Philippines this was the boldest and led to the most headshaking among the European colonial powers. Neither the French in Indochina, nor the Dutch in Indonesia, nor the British in their Asian possessions had ever plunged their subject-peoples into mass education, technical training, and political power. The Americans, by contrast, were in a hurry.

By 1907 they had authorized elections for the first Philip-pine Assembly. A new party, the Nacionalistas ("National-ists"), pledged to speedy and complete independence, swept the polls and dominated the new lower house. The Philip-pine Commission, with a majority of Americans, became the upper house and could, of course, checkmate any decisions of the lower chamber. But this limitation on self-government vanished in a few years. In 1913, when the Democrats under President Woodrow Wilson took control of the United

*The First Philippine Assembly, meeting after elections in
1907. The Philippine Senate still uses desks arranged like this.*

States Government, they appointed a majority of five Filipinos to four Americans in the upper house. And a new
Governor-General, Francis Burton Harrison, made it plain
that Washington intended the Filipinos to govern themselves
to the extent of their ability.

The wheels of self-rule spun faster. Under the Jones Act,
passed by the United States Congress in 1916, the Filipinos
moved closer to becoming virtual masters of their own
internal affairs. Now they had a new legislature, with a
Senate and a House of Representatives elected by "qualified"
—namely, propertied and educated—voters. They had a new
Cabinet in which Filipinos headed five of six departments,

and a pliable governor-general who held the veto power but used it rarely. The Supreme Court was still controlled by American judges, but the Philippines had moved fast, some Americans thought too fast, toward self-government.

When the Republicans regained power in Washington in 1921, they applied the brakes. Pointing to chaos in government finances, to 60,000 deaths from cholera and smallpox in a two-year period, to political interference with government departments, they concluded that government by Filipinos had been neither stable nor effective. General Leonard Wood, the new Republican Governor-General, soon vetoed so much legislation that he clashed with virtually every Filipino leader. The entire Cabinet resigned in protest. Until 1927, the end of his term, Wood governed on his own.

The results could have been foreseen. Like other authoritarian rulers before and since, Wood governed with energy and gave the regime an efficiency it had not known. He also rekindled Filipino defiance. Once cooperative leaders now joined the out-and-out nationalists in demanding full independence. Wood's successor, Henry L. Stimson, probably the ablest of all American governors of the Philippines, restored cooperation with the Filipinos but failed to stop the independence movement.

Prelude to Independence

Ironically, it was American businessmen and union leaders, not American idealists, who gave the cause of Filipino independence its final push to success. Philippine sugar, coconut oil and other products had had free entry into the American market since 1909. Low-paid Filipino labor competed with American, especially on the West Coast and in the Merchant Marine. When the great depression struck the

General Leonard Wood reading his annual message to the Philippine Congress in 1923. Manuel Quezon and Manuel Roxas, the two stony-faced men in the background, were quarreling with Wood. Both were later to be Presidents of the Philippines.

United States in 1929, sugar interests and high-tariff advocates saw an opportunity. An independent Philippines would cease to be a competitor; its goods could be shut out, like those of other foreign countries, by tariff walls.

Thus it was not noble motives which led the American Congress, late in the Administration of President Herbert Hoover, to approve a bill giving early freedom to the Philippines. The bill, however, called for the maintenance of American military and naval bases in the islands. On this ground, the Philippine legislature rejected it. A second attempt, the Tydings-McDuffie Act, succeeded in 1934, in the floodtide of Franklin Roosevelt's New Deal.

The new law, like the previous version, did not confer independence at once. It did something almost as daring: it set a timetable. The Filipinos would write their own constitution and elect their own government as quickly as possible. They were to set up a government to be known as the Commonwealth for a ten-year term. Defense, foreign affairs, tariffs, and the currency would remain under American control. Otherwise, the Filipinos would be virtually free to run their own affairs without American interference. By July 4, 1946, the Commonwealth would give way to a fully independent sovereign republic.

This transitional plan was a good deal less generous than the dominion status the British had granted South Africa in 1907, after the Boer War. However, it did give the Philippines more self-government than any Asian colony had yet achieved. The commonwealth device satisfied the Filipinos and the American liberals. For a time, it also satisfied the jealous American business interests and their Congressional spokesmen, for it seemed to assure the end of the free entry of Philippine products after ten years. But the end of free trade would have done the Philippines untold harm. American rule had made the colony so dependent on the American market that a tariff wall would have pauperized the new nation. By 1939, the United States had agreed to apply its tariffs only gradually over a twenty-year period. And even this threat to the Philippine economy was subsequently eased. (See pages 150 and 153–54.)

Well could President Franklin D. Roosevelt say in 1935 that "in the long run we have chosen the right course with respect to the Philippine Islands." Well could he praise the Filipinos for their patience during American rule, their willingness to adjust and adapt, and their devotion to free institutions. Patience may not always have been the mark of Filipino politicians during the American regime; repeatedly their tempers flared, their speeches grew shrill and defiant, as they prodded the Americans to move faster toward independence. But after the collapse of Aguinaldo's "insurrection," the Filipinos never again revolted. They did not need to. They came to trust the Americans and to believe American promises. Filipino nationalists had been devoted to free institutions, in theory, as early as 1898; this much they had learned from books and from their students' discoveries in Western Europe. Within a few years, however, their devotion to free institutions became deeper and more durable— through practice in making them work.

On the eve of launching the Commonwealth, Filipino leaders again proved that they had learned the theory and the mechanics of democratic self-government. Meeting for six months in 1934 and early 1935, elected Filipino delegates hammered out a new constitution. (See pages 119–20.) It gave the Philippines a more centralized government structure than that of the United States or of the revolutionary regime of 1898, but it borrowed many democratic forms from both. Filipino voters—those able to read and write—approved the constitution in a plebiscite. President Roosevelt, in March, 1935, certified that it was acceptable to the United States.

One more step remained for the Filipinos: to elect their new executive leaders and members of Congress. On November 15, 1935, while 250,000 Filipinos looked on, Manuel L. Quezon and Sergio Osmeña were sworn in as freely elected President and Vice-President, respectively, of the new Commonwealth. It was the proudest moment, up to that time, in the troubled history of Philippine nationalism.

THE NEW LEADERS

Here let us stop briefly to meet the two leaders who dominated Philippine politics in that watershed year of 1935.

*Manuel L. Quezon, who became first President of the
Philippine Commonwealth in 1935.*

Manuel Quezon, the new President, was neither a thinker
like Rizal nor a man of war like Aguinaldo. He was a
nationalist politician, of a type which was to become familiar
in Asia and Africa after World War II. Born in 1878 of a
part-Spanish family in southern Luzon, he fought with Aguinaldo against Spaniards and Americans. He won a law
degree after the "insurrection," and soon went into politics.

Nobody excelled young Quezon in the passion and fire of
his speeches. Repeatedly he took the simple stand of a
nationalist: he would, as he said, prefer "a government run
like hell by Filipinos to one run like heaven by the Americans." At the same time, he knew how to persuade in public

debate and in private talk. For these reasons he became, in 1909, the nonvoting Philippine delegate to the United States Congress.

There his wiry form, his piercing eyes, his vibrant voice became familiar to American politicians of both parties. Without a vote, he nevertheless played an effective part in passage of the Jones Act of 1916, which gave the Filipinos a large measure of internal self-government. From then until 1935 he served as President of the Philippine Senate, always keeping the goal of full independence before the Filipinos.

Unlike Quezon in origin and temperament was the Vice-President, Sergio Osmeña. His mixed heritage was part Chinese rather than part Spanish. From his Chinese ancestors he had inherited a shrewdness, a coolness in business and political dealings, which the more dramatic Quezon lacked. Osmeña came from Cebu, the largest city in the Visayan islands. He and his family had grown rich there, and he kept Cebuano votes and allegiance throughout his political life. He was, in other words, a perfect specimen of the local boss, a descendant of the old *caciques,* with whom both Spaniards and Americans cooperated in ruling the Philippines.

Osmeña was born in 1878, the same year as Quezon. He became speaker of the Assembly the same year Quezon entered national political life. The two were rivals, with Osmeña the dominant figure until the early 1920's. While Quezon always seemed to be playing a role on a stage, Osmeña was more the quiet manager behind the scenes. Yet under the Commonwealth the two found ways to cooperate and complement each other.

In normal times these men might have steered the new Commonwealth into smooth waters and safe harbors. But they never had the chance to do this. External dangers soon darkened the horizon. With a wary eye on Japan, President

Sergio Osmeña presiding over the first Philippine Assembly.

Quezon brought General Douglas MacArthur to Manila as his military adviser. The two proceeded to plan for a regular army of 10,000 men as a nucleus, and around it a reserve force of 40,000 new trainees each year. This would have given the Philippines 300,000 trained men by 1946, the year of independence.

Tokyo had a different timetable. The danger of Japanese attack was so apparent by July 1941 that President Roosevelt made the Commonwealth army a part of American forces and named MacArthur as the American commander in the Far East. Hurried preparations were far from adequate. On the day of Pearl Harbor, December 7, Japanese raiding planes smashed all the American planes on the ground at Clark Field north of Manila. A month later Manila had fallen, the Japanese had landed on all the major islands, and most of the American and Filipino forces were trapped on the mountainous Bataan Peninsula near the entrance to Manila Bay. The United States had failed to shield its Far Eastern possession. The Filipinos were fated to go through an ordeal of fire and blood before they could achieve their freedom.

The Philippines in World War II

The Japanese onslaught gave Filipinos a chance to turn on their former American masters, to side with Asian invaders against Westerners. But Filipino troops did not desert or betray. In the heroic defense of Bataan they fought well, side by side with the Americans, whom they outnumbered, and many died. The survivors, Filipino and American, shuffled off together and endured together the infamous "death march" to the Japanese stockades.

President Quezon and a few other leaders of the Commonwealth lived with General MacArthur and American civilians in the tunnels dug into the island rock of Corregidor. The American High Commissioner to the Philippines, Francis Bowes Sayre, has pictured the Corregidor drama in his book of reminiscences, *Glad Adventure:*

> We ate in relays at a common mess in the tunnel, slept in the tunnel, and carried on there as long as the foul air and difficult working conditions permitted. . . . President Quezon's cot was close to mine, and I could hear his racking cough through much of the night. He was a sick man, fighting his old enemy, tuberculosis, which finally took his life on August 1, 1944. . . . Our men were still so new to air attacks that casualties were heavy, and soon our hospital tunnel corridors were crowded with blood-soaked stretchers and dying men.

Under these grueling conditions, Quezon and Osmeña took the oaths of office for their second terms as President and Vice-President. They endured bombardment and fetid confinement in the tunnel for almost two months. Then, on the night of February 20, 1942, an American submarine took them to a temporary haven on the island of Negros, in the Visayas, not yet under full Japanese control.

Ultimately they reached the United States safely, and led their country from exile, as the leaders of many other invaded nations had done. Among those who escaped to Negros with them were Chief Justice José Abad Santos and Brigadier General Manuel Roxas, later to become President. The Chief Justice chose to stay on Negros; the Japanese caught him and shot him because he refused to break his oath of allegiance to the United States. In death he became a martyred hero.

Roxas, equally patriotic, decided to risk a return to Manila. Someone had to carry on civilian government, and Roxas believed he could help his people by staying with them. But by doing so he and hundreds of others came under suspicion as collaborators. In the Philippines, as in France and other occupied countries, politics during and after the war were bedeviled by the distinction between those who escaped and those who stayed, between those who obeyed the conquerors and those who fought them as guerrillas.

Two guerrilla movements tormented the Japanese throughout their years of military occupation. The first of them remained in touch by radio, submarine landings, and air drops with the government-in-exile and with General MacArthur's command. Filipino and American officers directed the daring work of sabotage, ambush, and espionage, especially in northern Luzon and the southern islands. Many of these secret fighters were caught, tortured, and shot. Some managed to escape, and a few survived to become popular leaders during the next twenty years. It became valuable for a vote-getter to carry the scars of Japanese imprisonment and torture.

The second of the guerrilla movements operated independently of the MacArthur campaign. Arising in the rice bowl of central Luzon, the scene of a peasant uprising in 1935, this one adopted the Tagalog name of *Hukbong Bayan Laban sa Hapon* ("People's Army to Fight the Japanese"). The Hukbalahaps (Huks), as they were called, had been founded with Communist help in the 1920's as a secret revolutionary movement. In wartime they fought in the hills against Japanese and landlords alike. They killed fewer Japanese than Filipinos; the anti-Japanese struggle was little more than a cover for their revolutionary work. They seized big estates, killed the owners, and handed land to those farmers who cooperated with them. (See pages 124–26.)

Meanwhile the vast majority of Filipinos, from leaders to the poorest farmers, had to submit to Japanese rule. What else could they have done? The Japanese were rigid and ruthless. They swept away the free institutions of the Commonwealth, wiped out the political parties, instituted censorship, requisitioned private property, and compelled the Filipinos to serve Japan's needs. City dwellers had to scrounge, cheat, and steal for food and clothing. The dreaded secret police, the Kempitei, made its headquarters at Fort Santiago. Many Filipinos suffered agony and death within its walls.

To carry out their purposes, the Japanese set up two successive puppet governments. The first, in 1942, was an executive commission with an advisory council of state. The second was an "independent" republic formed in October 1943, with José Laurel as its president. The republic showed

Manila's public buildings were blackened shells like these when the city was finally liberated, February 1945.

outer trappings of independence: a cabinet, a flag, an ambassador in Tokyo. Yet in every detail it remained subject to Japanese orders.

For the sorely tried Filipino people, MacArthur's landing on Leyte in October 1944 was only the beginning of the end of their purgatory. New destruction rained upon them and upon their already battered towns and farms. On many other islands where Americans and Filipinos landed, the Japanese pulled themselves together to fight the allied columns which were knifing their way inland. Their resistance reached a suicidal frenzy when American and Filipino forces drove toward Manila from the north and south at the start of 1945.

The Japanese, encircled ever more tightly in the capital city, chose to fight block by block, building by building, rather than surrender. In this long and bitter siege, some 60,000 civilians were killed, many of them murdered in cold blood by the Japanese. The walled section of Intramuros, with its churches and other landmarks dating from old Spanish days, became a desert of blackened walls and rubble. When the liberators finally cleared Manila of Japanese, it had become the worst devastated city of World War II except for Warsaw and Berlin.

Could the Philippines have escaped these horrors by becoming independent and neutral in 1935? Some Filipinos, notably the brilliant constitutional lawyer, Senator Claro M. Recto, thought so. Even President Quezon once considered the idea of neutralization. At the darkest moment of the war, when he was fighting for breath in the Corregidor tunnels, he lost heart. He felt the United States had betrayed his people by failing to save them from the Japanese. With General MacArthur's approval, he sent President Roosevelt a message asking immediate independence and an agreement with Japan to neutralize the Philippines. Roosevelt, shocked, answered that the United States had not broken faith. "The present sufferings of the Filipino people, cruel as they are," he told Quezon, "are infinitely less than the sufferings and permanent enslavement which will inevitably follow acceptance of Japanese promises." Quezon quickly changed his mind. He agreed that the Philippines would fight to the end.

In any event, it was not in the Filipino nature to knuckle under to a foreign invader, as Aguinaldo had proved. Neutral or not, independent or American-controlled, Filipinos would not have risked their religious, cultural, and economic ties with the West to embrace Japan's Greater East Asia Co-Prosperity Sphere. The Islands had long been Japanese targets in the plans of Tokyo militarists to drive Western influence from Asia. A settlement of 17,000 Japanese at Davao, in the southern island of Mindanao, had served as a potent fifth column. (See page 148.) Probably, therefore, the Philippines could not have escaped being overrun by the Japanese, although they might have avoided much death and destruction by surrender.

President Quezon did not live to see what his people everywhere joyfully welcomed as liberation. His eight years in office expired in 1943, but the United States Congress lengthened his term until after the war. On August 1, 1944, he died of tuberculosis at Saranac Lake, New York, knowing only that MacArthur's forces were nearing the Philippines from New Guinea. It was his Vice-President and successor, Sergio Osmeña, who waded ashore with MacArthur at Leyte and reestablished the Commonwealth Government on Filipino soil.

Osmeña showed breadth of mind toward those Filipinos who had served in civilian posts under the Japanese. The Americans were less magnanimous. As soon as they could get their hands on members of the puppet government, they arrested and jailed all of them except Roxas. Senator Recto, chairman of the constitutional convention of 1934–35, was among those jailed. He could not get a flicker of recognition from MacArthur when the Allied Commander visited his prison. The Administration in Washington demanded that Osmeña rid his government of collaborators. The resulting bitterness poisoned Philippine politics and relations between the Philippines and the United States in the year that remained before the scheduled independence.

The first postwar election took place on April 23, 1946. Whoever won was to manage the Commonwealth in its last weeks, and then take charge of the independent Republic. Osmeña ran for reelection as President, but as we shall see later, he was defeated by Manuel Roxas as head of a new party, the Liberals.

Thus the leader who had gone into exile in the United States was retired to private life, and the one who had chosen to stay behind under the Japanese became President. On July 4, 1946, a vast crowd jammed the Luneta, the bayside park in Manila where Rizal had been shot almost fifty years before. Paul V. McNutt, the United States High Commissioner, hauled down the Stars and Stripes, Roxas raised the Philippine flag, and the long struggle for Philippine independence was ended.

But it was a saddened and crippled land which faced the world as a free nation. The war had been a triple disaster, in terms of lives lost, of property destroyed, and of political unity shattered. Of the hundreds of thousands of Filipinos who had died in the struggle, many were the bravest and the best, equipped to give leadership to their country. The destruction of property and resources brought the Philippines into nationhood as a virtual pauper, wholly dependent, as we shall see, on the United States. Finally, the cooperation of some Filipinos with the Japanese, and of others with the Americans, made the conduct of postwar politics difficult when both groups had to work together.

Political Institutions

No other country, except perhaps modern Greece, gives politics such inexhaustible attention. Both social chatter and serious argument revolve endlessly around the choice of candidates, the shifts of allegiances, the search for votes, the prospects of election, and the inevitable post-election scandals. The political merry-go-round is a sporting and gambling event, like a continuous cockfight and stock market session combined. It is also a deeply serious business, for politics in the Philippines is a road to wealth and power. This helps to explain why so many of the ablest Filipinos, especially the top graduates of the law schools, make politics their life work. The urge to do something for one's kinfolk or oneself is more compelling, with exceptions, than the urge to do something for one's country.

117

Elections are only the recurrent climaxes of a serial story that has no end. Political campaigns run to inordinate length. The candidates in the November 1965 presidential election, for example, won formal nominations a year earlier, and the struggle for each party's nomination had seesawed for a year before that. Philippine campaigns are longer than the combined primary and election campaigns in an American Presidential year. This surely gives the Filipino public a world's record for endurance. During an election year, every government's policy-making is virtually paralyzed.

To say all this is not to denigrate the Filipinos or their system. On the contrary, almost alone among newly-independent peoples, the Filipinos have kept their trust in the ballot. Their opposition works from the political platform and the polling place. It does not have to languish in jail or shoot from the jungle, except for a few hundred die-hard rebels in central Luzon and in the southern islands.

To the Filipinos' credit stands one other record. They have never had a dictator. They have never turned to a professional military man as their savior. The armed forces have never conspired to put one of their leaders into the highest office in the land. In the thirty-odd years since the Commonwealth gave Filipinos control of their own affairs, no government has had to put down an attempted *coup d'etat* (except, of course, the one produced by the Japanese invasion). Anyone who writes off the Philippines as just an Asian "banana republic" should consider this thought well. Filipinos have transferred power solely by legal means, and twice since 1946 have shifted power peacefully from the ruling party to its opponents. They have shown a continuing respect for the constitutional limits of civilian power. How many other nations in present-day Asia, Africa, and Latin America can meet this standard?

A Centralized System

The Philippine Constitution looks, at first sight, almost like a carbon copy of that of the United States. Even its preamble rings with Jeffersonian prose, for its goals are "to promote the general welfare" and to secure for all the people "the blessings of independence under a regime of justice, liberty and democracy." It provides, among other things, for a President and Vice-President elected for four years, with reelection up to a maximum of eight; a Congress composed of a Senate of 24 members and a House of Representatives of 104, the former elected for six years, the latter for four; an independent judiciary, with a Supreme Court empowered to review the constitutionality of executive and legislative acts; an independent national auditing office; a bill of rights as sweeping as any civil libertarian could wish; and subordination of the armed forces to a civilian President as Commander-in-Chief.

CONTRASTS WITH THE UNITED STATES

Actually, the Philippine system is more centralized than the American. The Congress holds plenary legislative powers; that is, it can do anything not expressly forbidden by the Constitution. All Senators are elected at large; their constituency, therefore, is national. The President and Congress do not have to yield certain powers to state governors and legislatures—for the simple reason that "sovereign" states, in the American sense, do not exist.

The Philippines has 56 provinces, each with its elected governor, but they are little more than historical and geographical abstractions. The governors are local agents of the national leaders. They cannot draw on local taxes, for all taxes are national except, since 1963, for those levied by the village councils for local use. A provincial governor cannot, for example, initiate or administer a farm extension system, or rural health services, or intermediate education. He cannot appoint a treasurer, assessor, health officer, or other essentially local functionaries, or even the teachers in the intermediate schools. All such appointments must be made by the national government. The progressive Senator Raul Manglapus, long a battler for decentralized government, complained early in 1965 that "even the building of schoolhouses and bandstands and basketball courts must depend on the will of the men who sit at the capital." An energetic city mayor finds that he must always go to "Manila"—meaning to his congressman or to his national administration—for the smallest outlay of funds for civic improvement. "Manila" keeps firm control. For all the provinces and municipalities in the Philippines, "Manila" sets aside only 12 per cent of its inadequate internal revenue collections. The percentage is simply too small to be divided among so many claimants.

There are at least three reasons for this centralized system. First, both the Spanish and American regimes were always strongly centralized. Second, the present Constitution was written in 1935, when an imperious leader, Quezon, held political sway. He did not want the President or members of Congress to share power with state governors and legislatures, as in the American system. The third, often cited by Quezon's defenders, was the unsettled state of international relations at the time. All too apparent were the militaristic conquests on which Japan had already embarked, the rise of Hitler and Mussolini in Europe, and the inability of many parliamentary regimes to defend themselves. In the light of World War II and its aftermath, who can say Quezon was wrong?

Parties and Interests

The Philippine Constitution, like the American, makes no mention of political parties. This is common sense, for Philippine parties have little meaning except as mechanisms for getting elected. In the first decade of American rule, parties did reflect a point of view on one issue: independence. The Americans first fostered a single puppet party, the Federalista, which was content with American tutelage. In 1907, as we have seen, a genuine nationalist party, the Nacionalista, arose to challenge the United States, and swept the first Assembly election. It stood for complete independence, and remained the virtually undisputed master of Philippine politics until the end of World War II.

Then only, for the first time, the Philippines developed a two-party system, at least in name. Manuel Roxas, who had remained in the Islands during the Japanese regime, broke from the Nacionalista President Osmeña, who had spent most of the war in the United States. Roxas formed a new party, the Liberals, and proceeded to trounce Osmeña, becoming the first President of an independent Philippines.

Like the Republican and Democratic parties in the United States, the Nacionalistas and the Liberals are coalitions made up of many diverse elements. They care little about a consistent ideology. A Philippine party tends to elevate, surround, and follow a leader who has shown that he can win votes; and the voters, by and large, make their choices on personalities rather than issues. The two Philippine parties have therefore been described as factions rather than genuine parties, and with some reason. Professor Renato E. Agpalo, chairman of the Department of Political Science at the University of the Philippines, has called the two parties "loose, fissiparous aggregations of leaders of big families and interest groups" such as planters, manufacturers, small merchants, farmers, and many others.

"The two," he says, "have practically the same economic, social and political values. It is not unusual for either party to lose top leaders, as well as ordinary members, to the other party. Every now and then both are threatened by or give birth to short-lived third parties. In other words, neither party is powerful enough to make its members and leaders follow the party line. Most of the time, members of the party quarrel over party spoils."

In such a system the lobbyist has become a political institution in his own right. President Quezon learned all about lobbying when he served as the nonvoting delegate to the United States Congress, and his successors have proceeded to improve on what he learned. By now Filipinos have built lobbying into a high or low political art. Among the interests which compete for favors are the landowning families, which fight land reform; the sugar and other exporters, who seek a continuing share of the vast American market; the big and small businessmen, who want to stamp out competition from the Chinese living in the Philippines; and the Chinese manufacturers and merchants, organized into the well-financed Federation of Chinese Chambers of Commerce. All these groups seek to make congressmen and even Presidents beholden to them. Among the newer interests are the labor unions, who are beginning to be powerful in the cities, and the intellectuals, who seek to raise the standards of Philippine political life. Only the masses of farmers are, as yet, without an effective lobby—but their day will come.

The lobbyists' tasks are made easier by the fluid political system. A Filipino politician is not tied irrevocably to any party or any set of beliefs. So vast is the centralized patronage and "pork" dispensed by the President, and by his party members in Congress, that local officials of the out-of-power party often switch allegiance in order to survive. After one party has won an election and the patronage that goes with it, members of the defeated party tend to defect to insure jobs and public funds for their districts. When an in-power party seems to be losing public support, the defections often go the other way, as we shall see; officeholders often desert the government, hoping to come in on the ground floor when the opposition returns to power. This kind of defection occurs even at the top of the political structure. Thus Vice-President Emmanuel Pelaez, in 1964, deserted the Liberals who had made him their heir apparent. The Liberal Senate President Ferdinand Marcos, to take another example, not only switched in the same way, but in 1964 proceeded to win the Nacionalistas' nomination for President.

The story of Philippine politics under the Republic, then, is one of leaders rather than parties. An understanding of Philippine politics requires a look at the political record of these men in the generation since independence.

The Leaders

FROM ROXAS TO MAGSAYSAY

The Republic's first President, Manuel Roxas, had a short and troubled term in office. He did manage to get the national government staffed and functioning again, and to mop up the worst of the war's material debris. What dominated his term was the search for economic aid, tariff preferences, and military protection from the United States. (See pages 150–51 and 206.) In the struggle to survive, the new nation had no time under Roxas to tackle long-term Philippine problems. The Republic, although technically independent, was still wholly, gallingly dependent on the United States when Roxas died of a heart attack in April 1948.

His successor as Liberal leader and President was his Vice-President, Elpidio Quirino. A former secretary to Quezon in the prewar years, a guerrilla fighter against the Japanese, he was a rarity in the top rank of Filipino politicians: a self-made man who had worked his way through law school. His background suggested that he was what the Philippines needed. The time was overripe for a leader of the whole people, one who could heal wartime wounds and rally the entire nation to renewal and reform.

This, however, was not to be. Taking office in a war-shattered country, Quirino could not even hold his own party, much less his nation, together. He was reelected by a narrow margin in 1949 in what still, in 1965, ranked and rankled as the most corrupt campaign and election in Philippine annals. Quirino was personally honest; in his full term he began to make headway against inflation, waste, favoritism, and inefficiency in government. But the fundamental evils, especially the deepening misery of the small farmers, remained unchecked.

Internal revolt as well as economic distress racked the Philippines in the Quirino years. Rebels of the Hukbalahap movement (see page 112) had emerged in Roxas' brief term as an open opposition movement. Their leader, Luis Taruc, nominally a socialist, had been elected to Congress in 1946, but by 1948 the government had discovered his Communist connections and support. When Roxas outlawed the movement in 1948, Taruc fled and resumed the wartime guerrilla struggle in central Luzon. Again the Huks killed landlords and seized and burned their properties. In 1949 they were so callous as to murder President Quezon's widow, her daughter, and her son-in-law in an ambush.

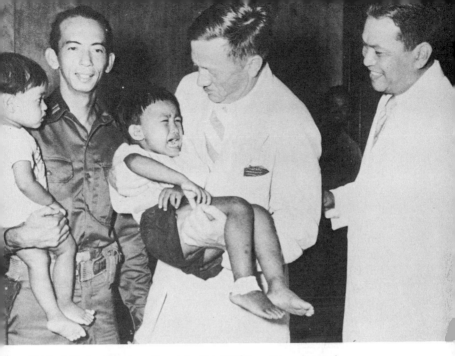

*United States Supreme Court Justice William Douglas and
a Philippine army captain hold children abandoned by the
Huks during a surprise raid on one of their strongholds.
Defense Secretary Ramón Magsaysay, on the right, smiles
reassuringly. The children were cared for by the government.*

It must not be assumed that the simple farmers who hid,
fed, and sheltered the Huks were Communists. The Huks
were revolting against genuine social grievances which nobody else was trying, seriously, to remove. Rice farmers were
still paying more than half of their crops to absentee landowners, and protested against such conditions. The Communists simply attached themselves to this protest movement,
skillfully exploited it, and to a large extent encouraged and
directed it for their own ends. The Huk regulars never
exceeded 10,000 men. The far larger mass of their sympa-

thizers wanted relief; the Communists wanted control, not only of central Luzon but of the national government itself.

In the Quirino years they came uncomfortably close to winning it. The Philippine army and constabulary, clustered in the towns, riddled with favoritism and graft among their officers, could make no headway against the rebels. Cruel methods of suppression only added to peasant bitterness. Finally, in 1951, the harassed Quirino took American advice and appointed a remarkable 43-year-old ex-guerrilla and Congressman, Ramón Magsaysay, as Secretary of Defense. This, the finest of Quirino's decisions, turned the tide against the Huks. It also brought the long-sought winds of reform blowing through the Philippines.

THE MAGSAYSAY PHENOMENON

Ramón Magsaysay looked, talked, and acted like a man of the people. He lacked the surface smoothness of many Filipino politicians, especially of those with partly Spanish or Chinese ancestry. To some extent his manner was deceptive. His father owned a furniture factory, and his family owned four square miles of land. But, unlike other landlords' scions, he knew how to work with his hands. A big, broad-shouldered man, he gave his people the impression of being a genial giant, a kind of Paul Bunyan, without fear and without nerves.

He quickly showed that he was a man of ideas as well as energy. To defeat the Huks, it was not enough to regroup the army and get it away from the towns into the countryside. It

A reformed Huk guerrilla poses with his family outside his new home in Mindanao. Fewer than 300 took the offer of new land.

was not enough to kill or capture the Huks in their small and scattered bands. The army also had to win the farmers to its side and ultimately to make friends of the Huks themselves.

To win the farmers, Magsaysay ordered the army to help with civil works: with digging wells, harvesting crops, combating floods, building schools. To win the Huks, Magsaysay offered not only an amnesty to each one who surrendered, but also twenty-five acres and a house in underdeveloped, underpopulated Mindanao. These were revolutionary methods of fighting a rebellion. They worked. Only about 250 Huks accepted the offer of new land, but thousands of others slipped back into peaceful and law-abiding lives. By 1953 the policy of "all-out friendship, all-out force" had reduced the Huks to a hard core of a few hundred hiding in the Luzon hills. It was the first time in post-World War II Asia that a free country had pulled the fangs of a Communist-inspired revolt.

A presidential election lay in the offing in early 1953. Politicians of the opposition Nacionalista party showed increasing interest in Magsaysay's personality, energy, and popular appeal. What if he was a novice in politics? He could win the votes, and the professionals could ride to power on his shirttails. So Magsaysay was persuaded to do what Roxas had done in 1946: to break with his leader and run for the Presidency.

Magsaysay's election campaign as the Nacionalista candidate was as unorthodox as his fight against the Huks. For the first time a contender for the highest office actually courted the farmer in the *barrios*. He spoke in province after province, village after village, talking, handshaking, and picnicking with the people. Promising reform, denouncing corruption, extolling the virtues of the long-exploited peasants, he won a landslide victory over Quirino and his badly

*In his favorite informal attire, the loose, untucked
shirt, Magsaysay liked to ignore security measures and
mingle freely with the people.*

divided Liberals. In contrast with the disgraces of four years
earlier, it was the cleanest, most peaceful election the Philippines had known.

As President, Magsaysay cheerfully smashed other traditions. Using his executive powers to the limit, he set up a
Court of Agrarian Relations, to handle the grievances of
individual sharecroppers. He began community development
in the *barrios*. (See pages 168–69.) In Malacañang Palace
itself, the residence of Spanish and American governors and

Filipino Presidents, he set up an office where anyone, even the poorest illiterate farmer, could complain without fear of reprisal. The humblest citizen now had some recourse against the bureaucrat.

On stated days a long line of citizens, many of them barefooted, entered the palace, delivered their complaints, and heard them courteously received. Often the President himself listened to their tales of trouble. Perhaps a local police chief had unjustly harassed a stallholder in the market; perhaps a soldier had damaged a farmer's house or land. Whatever the grievance, Magsaysay not only heard it but acted, first to investigate, and then to deal with the trouble.

In one sense this was a return to an old Asian tradition by which rulers, like alms-givers, had let their poor subjects petition for redress. But Magsaysay was no alms-giver in attitude or method. He somehow made the petitioners feel he was one of them. He gave them the sense that the government was on their side. Nothing like this had been seen in the Philippines.

A relatively young President of forty-five, he brought still younger men into executive positions. Some of these newcomers, "Magsaysay's boys," were to remain gadflies and reformers in politics for more than a decade: Manuel Manahan, Raul Manglapus, Emmanuel Pelaez, later to become Vice-President, and many others. Like both the Roosevelts who gained the American Presidency, Magsaysay quickened the interest of masses of people in government.

His actual accomplishments were less impressive than the invigoration he gave to Philippine political life. Much of what the country needed he advocated: land reform, labor unionization, economic planning, and anti-corruption laws. But Congress and the courts still obeyed entrenched interests. Only a superb political tactician could have made headway against them. Among Magsaysay's many gifts, the art of persuasion by political give-and-take was not one. Toward the end of his first term the momentum of his administration had slackened. Most of his reforms had been blocked. He needed another four years to achieve them, and then more years in which his lieutenants could carry on.

He never had the chance to do this. On a visit to Cebu in 1957, his plane crashed into a hillside, and he, the masses' idol, lay dead. His Vice-President, Carlos P. García, a smooth and shrewd Nacionalista of the old school, stepped into the Presidency.

Some of "Magsaysay's boys" formed a third party in the hope of enacting the late President's program. Their hope was not to win but to take away enough votes to defeat García in his bid for a full term. Under Manuel Manahan, who had been in charge of Magsaysay's Complaints Commission, the third party failed. García won in a bitter and noisy campaign, and the politicians in Manila resumed their old ways.

But reform was not quite dead. For in the 1957 election the voters did something brand-new in Philippine politics. They not only elected García, the Nacionalista, as President, but to García's astonishment and anger, they also elected a young Liberal, Diosdado Macapagal, as Vice-President. Macapagal was a self-made lawyer, diplomat, and Congressman and the son of a poor tenant farmer. By their ticket-splitting the voters had shown a new independence and maturity. No longer did they assume that "they (the *caciques,* or local bosses) know what's best for us." They were beginning to think for themselves.

Why and how have young leaders like Magsaysay and his "boys" risen to prominence, although they did not spring from the wealthy landowning class? How could the self-made Quirino and the struggling son of a sharecropper, Macapagal, become Presidents of the Republic? One obvious answer is education. There is no class barrier to a law degree, and a law degree, in turn, opens the doors to a political career. But there are other, less obvious, explanations.

One is that political bosses in the Philippines, as elsewhere, want a winner as a candidate for high office. The old, established families will gladly support an outsider for election as mayor, governor, or even President if he shows vote-getting power. The old families used to think they could control such newcomers, as they controlled the unhappy President Quirino, and as they hoped they could manage or checkmate Magsaysay. Nowadays, however, the monopoly of the "establishment" is by no means as tight as formerly. The spread of literacy and voting in the *barrios,* the new legal safeguards against the padding of electoral rolls and the outright buying of votes—all these have put the old families on the defensive. Clearly other poor boys will rise to the Presidency, and some day one of these outsiders will master the "establishment" at last.

THE MACAPAGAL "NEW ERA"

In the Philippine system, as we have seen, a President holds vast powers. Quezon had seen to that long ago. President García, who knew his Constitution, proceeded to use his powers as if his Vice-President did not exist. He denied Macapagal the usual perquisite of an office in Malacañang Palace; he even refused him the use of an official car. García knew all the arts of winning support from powerful leaders of Congress. He permitted Magsaysay's few tangible reforms, like community development, to continue; but he did not believe in the need of further changes The main accom-

Diosdado Macapagal (center) and his family as guests of the United States' First Family in Washington.

plishments of his Presidency lay in the field of foreign affairs.

Macapagal, by contrast, had studied history and knew the history of the Magsaysay years. An intellectual by nature, or, as his detractors said, a pseudo-intellectual, he preferred reading history or biography in bed at four in the morning to standing on a political platform or shaking hands with the voters. Nevertheless, remembering Magsaysay, he set out to court the village voters. He traveled to every province and to many of the tiny islands. Although he had not been one of "Magsaysay's boys," he championed the farmer, denounced the García regime as corrupt, and promised a "new era" of justice and reform.

His effort paid off. The disowned Vice-President became a political force in his own right. Winning the Liberal nomination in 1961, he campaigned even more widely than Magsaysay had done. He knew, as García did not, that local bosses could no longer be sure of delivering the votes of the small farmer. He proceeded to defeat García by a narrow margin, with impressive help from rural voters.

Politics sank to unexampled bitterness during Macapagal's term. Businessmen, by and large, had no use for him except for the favors he might bestow. "Magsaysay's boys" did not wholly trust him, although his Vice-President, Emmanuel Pelaez, was one of them. The defeated President, García, was unforgiving. The night before he left office he appointed 350 of his own Nacionalista party to government posts.

The new administration thus ran into squalls even before clearing port. The voters had made navigation difficult for Macapagal: they had given him a Congress with both houses controlled by the opposition party. In time the President won a shaky numerical control by the classic Philippine methods of inducing defections. But in his first four years he never really mastered Congress. His high-minded speeches, his appeals to patriotism, his championship of the lowly and dispossessed, won him few votes in Congress and a drumfire of criticism in the Manila press. Because the Constitution limits regular Congressional sessions to 100 days a year, Macapagal had to resort to the weapon of calling special sessions. Trying to put through a land reform law (see pages 162–63), he had to summon six special sessions before he got it enacted in August, 1963. By then it was riddled with amendments and loopholes.

Much of the political bitterness stemmed from a sensational scandal known as the Stonehill case. During the García years and earlier, a former American serviceman named Harry S. Stonehill had fashioned a chain of interlocking enterprises in tobacco, real estate, and other businesses. He had become rich and powerful. He was on friendly terms with important figures in both parties.

One of his associates "squealed" to the government. In March 1962 Macagagal ordered Stonehill arrested and his records seized. These records showed that Stonehill had evaded taxes, bribed revenue agents, and contributed to the campaign funds of individuals in both parties. His records included a list of names of those whose palms he had greased. This list was a virtual "Who's Who" of Philippine politics and civil service.

In April the "squealer" was murdered mysteriously at sea. In August, the Macapagal government deported Stonehill as "an immediate and continuing menace" to the Republic. The opposition promptly cried that Macapagal was afraid to bring Stonehill to trial. The President added to the clamor by implicating his Vice-President, Pelaez, who angrily broke with him.

Corruption in Philippine politics did not, of course, begin or end with Stonehill. Under the traditional kinship system (see pages 173–74), a rich and powerful Filipino is obliged to help a poor relative, however distant the family connection may be. In wartime, under the Japanese, stealing became commonplace, and a new class of war profiteers emerged like rats from the ruins. To these traditions and habits, the postwar years added new opportunities. Black marketing, bribery, vote-buying, and smuggling seeped like poison gas through Philippine politics. Smuggling, in particular, became a big industry, its existence known to all. By 1964 it was estimated that the government was losing at least $50 million a year in tax revenues through the illegal landings of foreign goods. Every president denounced the evil, yet not one of them proved able to stamp it out.

By arresting Stonehill and by exhibiting a continuous show of activity against grafters and smugglers, President Macapagal did not make his legislative tasks easier. Not only Congress but the Supreme Court blunted the edge of his program. Repeatedly the court struck down the President's acts as unconstitutional. In some ways it was a repetition of Franklin D. Roosevelt's court setbacks early in the American New Deal. It also gave Macapagal a chance to repeat the tactics of Harry S. Truman during the 80th Congress in the United States. In the mid-term election of 1963, Macapagal went to the voters to denounce the "obstructionism" of Congress, while his enemies campaigned against him as a "dictator."

In all this record of forward movement accompanied by backsliding, three hopeful trends have emerged. One, as we have seen, is the new attention paid by "Manila" at campaign-time to the mass of underprivileged voters in the rural

A policeman catches a suspected smuggler of cigarettes, in the government's recurring but ineffective efforts to halt illegal imports.

villages. Another is the voters' growing independence, evident from the time of Magsaysay on, and demonstrated by the ticket-splitting of recent years. The third is the first faint tendency to vote on issues rather than personalities. In 1965 it was too early to say that these trends were more than temporary. But they were, at least, hints of change, and without change the Philippine political system, grafted by the United States onto a country inexperienced in democracy, was bound to fail.

Defective Structures

Fortunately, Filipinos are not so nationalistic that they cannot see the defects of their political institutions. President Macapagal, in particular, has urged Congress to call a constitutional convention to make changes. The present basic law, he said early in 1963, "partakes of the nature of a colonial constitution in the sense that it was adopted during the time of the Commonwealth and that it could not take effect without the approval of another country." Up to 1965 Congress refused. But criticism continued.

The critics, led by the President, have trained their fire on three political institutions: on Congress, for allegedly enriching and entrenching itself at the taxpayers' expense; on the courts, for making justice too slow and costly; and on the office of the President, for keeping too much centralized power.

Outwardly the Congress remains the most "colonial" of all the structures built by the 1935 Constitution. It is, as we have seen, modeled on the American Congress. At the opening of a session the President comes to the House chamber to deliver a state-of-the-nation address to members of both houses. In front of the rostrum, as in the United States, sit members of the Supreme Court and the Cabinet. In the side galleries are the diplomats, provincial governors, city mayors, and department heads. The public gallery is jammed (it always seems to be crowded in the Philippine Congress) with standees as well as seatholders.

In the Senate an American might easily imagine himself on Capitol Hill, except for two differences: the Vice-President does not preside, and the desks are arranged in a rectangular block instead of in a semicircle. The senators not only sit at desks which copy the old-fashioned schoolroom desks of their American counterparts, but they even copy the mannerisms of American senators, strolling around the chamber, whispering to colleagues, reading, or writing while a debate drones on. The committee structure, too, is taken directly from that of the United States Congress.

The criticisms of Congress are not directed at these Americanisms. President Macapagal and a section of the press have campaigned, rather, against a system of secret Congressional allowances which makes each member a powerful dispenser of funds. The 1935 Constitution gives each member only 7,200 pesos a year, or about $1,850 at the current rate of exchange. It also allows traveling expenses only when attending Congressional sessions.

Obviously legislators cannot live or carry on their work on such salaries. Therefore Congress has appropriated its own operating funds, out of which each member gets an unvouchered allowance. These appropriations have shot up in recent years; those for the House were almost twelve times as much in 1965 as in 1955. It has been estimated that each member's allowance averages 150,000 pesos (not quite $38,500). Each senator gets about five times as much. In addition, each congressman receives an allocation of money for public works in his district.

Naturally a congressman needs some of his allowance for maintaining an office. The average Congressional staff in 1965 was six, and this is not enough in a country where constituents besiege every legislator for favors. Yet the system of extra-legal unvouchered allowances has, without doubt, helped many a congressman to entrench himself politically in his own district. A congressman can do many kinds of vote-getting favors without brazenly buying votes for cash. He can provide government jobs, fat contracts, and legal help for constituents; he can see that roads, docks, clinics, or moneymaking enterprises come to his district; or in traditional Filipino style, he can simply feed large numbers of his constituents on festive occasions. Sometimes he dispenses these favors through the local political boss, sometimes he does it directly. He expects his reward to come on election day, and it usually does. In calling for reform of Congress, President Macapagal probably is beating his head against a stone wall.

Criticism of the judiciary is directed at the snail's pace of justice. Athough the Philippines boasts an overabundance of legal talent, it suffers from a shortage of courts, judges, and law libraries. At the start of 1963 the courts of first instance had accumulated a backlog of almost 83,000 cases, and the number of cases settled in the previous year did not even match the number of new cases filed. The inevitable delays mean that justice is not only slow but costly. In President Macapagal's words, the present delays in civil cases may not matter to a rich litigant, but "may very well mean the difference between life and death" to a poor wage-earner seeking relief.

The Philippine Congress has tended generally to support the status quo. It has opposed reform of its own structure and of the judicial system. Above all, it has killed most proposals to decentralize the Philippine political system. The one important exception to this negativism has been the creation of self-government, with local taxing powers, in the rural villages. But even this reform was political in its motivation.

The Barrio Councils

During the eventful Magsaysay term, in 1956, the national Congress finally set up a system of democratic elections for *barrio,* or village, councils. These councils, however, held only advisory powers, and Congress appropriated no money to finance them. Predictably, the experiment did not work. Villagers were reluctant to go to the polls, and did not understand a democratic system which was outside all their tradition and experience. Even after six years of trial, only half the eligible voters bothered to make their choice for councilmen.

But the young progressives who entered politics with Magsaysay pushed ahead with village reforms. Emmanuel Pelaez, who became Vice-President in 1961, made this his major task. Finally, in 1963, Congress passed amendments which gave the *barrio* councils real power. Since no national funds were available for village public works, village councils won the right, almost revolutionary in the Philippines, to levy local taxes. They were also allowed to receive 10 per cent of all real estate taxes collected in the villages.

Under the present "Barrio Charter," 28,687 village governments have been organized. The voters, who must be literate and twenty-one or over, constitute the *barrio* assembly. They elect the council, headed by a *barrio* lieutenant. The assembly, a kind of town meeting, meets only once a year. The council, however, meets monthly. Out of local taxes it can build and maintain local roads, bridges, water supplies and irrigation works. It can also set up cooperatives in farming, fishing and cottage industries; organize adult education programs; and employ community development workers. As for the *barrio* lieutenant, he is responsible for public order and fire protection and is charged with enforcement of laws within his village.

Genuine self-rule in the villages appears at last to have broken the age-old political apathy of the farmers. In 1964, for example, almost 400,000 individuals filed certificates as candidates for *barrio* council posts, and about 80 per cent of the eligible voters went to their village polls. But this interest has been won at a price.

It was the hope of Vice-President Pelaez and others of "Magsaysay's boys" that national politics would not intrude upon *barrio* democracy. Accordingly, the first slates of village candidates bore nonpolitical labels like the "Barrio Progress Party" or the "Cooperative Party." But such nonpartisanship did not suit the national parties. If village candidates could wear the Nacionalista or Liberal party labels, might not the winners deliver votes for congressmen and senators in national elections? So, seeing a shining opportunity, the national parties proceeded to organize the *barrios*. National issues threatened, in time, to dominate the local polls and to confuse the debate over local issues.

To sum up, Philippine political institutions contain many defects, as this chapter has shown. But they also provide the machinery for their own correction. The hope of correction springs from the continuing vigor of the Magsaysay legend, from the rise of an educated middle class in the cities, and from the inevitable growth of political consciousness among the farmers. Once the farmers know their own political power, they will surely force political changes. Yet it is not the faults of the political system that endanger the future of the Philippine Republic. The more serious dangers lurk within the misshapen economic institutions inherited from colonial rule. These we shall now examine.

Economic Institutions

The Philippine people have learned to their sorrow and frustration that economic independence does not necessarily go hand in hand with political freedom. Twenty years after winning its freedom, the new nation was still burdened with a colonial-type economy. This meant a predominantly agricultural economy. Farming employed more than 60 per cent of the work force, and earned more than a third of the national income. Industry still employed only 12 per cent of the work force, and accounted for less than a sixth of the national income.

With agriculture as its major economic institution, the nation could not feed itself, even on a low level of subsistence. It habitually imported something like a quarter of its food needs each year. One reason for the food deficit at home was the emphasis on crops grown for export. On three of these crops—sugar, coconuts, and abaca—the nation depended for almost two-thirds of its foreign exchange earnings.

This was not the kind of economic system associated with independence nor one the new nation proposed to tolerate indefinitely. For one thing, it was a hangover of colonialism and therefore humiliating. The Filipinos' national pride, as well as common sense, told them they should not depend so heavily for their living on one foreign market or one single country. Moreover, the system, they knew, harbored a built-in design for poverty at the broad base of the economic structure and for concentrated wealth at the pinnacle. And finally, the system has blocked the road to the kind of national growth which was both an economic and a political necessity.

In their precolonial centuries, the islanders had carried on a lively trade with China, Borneo, the empires of Java and Sumatra, and even India. Suddenly these old ties were cut. Almost everything the colony could produce flowed in the opposite direction, first to Spain and then, in growing volume, to the United States.

The Economics of Dependence

PRE-WORLD WAR II

Not all colonies were acquired for their wealth, but most of them ended up as suppliers of raw materials to the mother country. Thus Britain shaped Malaya; the Netherlands, Indonesia; and Japan, Korea and Manchuria to their own economic needs.

The United States varied the pattern somewhat. Soon after the conquest of the Philippines, American investors

Harvesting sugar cane, the Philippines' most important export crop, on the island of Negros.

were eager to obtain concessions of land and stake out claims to mineral resources. If they had had their way, the colonial economy would have developed along the same lines as those of the French in Indochina and the British in Malaya, with foreign-owned plantations and mines operated by "coolie" labor. American authorities rejected the classic pattern. One of their earliest decisions, under strong Filipino pressure, reserved the land and what might be under it to the people of the islands. Soon after, however, Congress heeded the voice of American industry and offered inducements to Filipino growers to develop their crops. The Payne Tariff of 1909 admitted Philippine products duty-free. The Underwood Tariff of 1913 established quotas on these products. One immediate reaction in the Philippines was the upgrading of cane sugar and the opening of a sugar mill in 1910.

Thus sugar quickly became the most important export crop and the major cause of economic dependence on the United States. The Philippines had begun to forge this bond even before it was made a dependent of Washington. During the last quarter of the nineteenth century, the United States became the principal sugar market of the Spanish colony, and by 1885 American refineries were already buying two-thirds of the Philippine crop. In that year, the total export crop amounted to about 225,000 short tons; by 1934, the colony was exporting 1,270,000 short tons, every bit of it to the United States. In that year, sugar accounted for 59 per cent of Philippine exports. It was also the year of the Tydings-McDuffie Act, scheduling independence for 1946, at which time Philippine products would no longer enter the United States duty-free. Small wonder that Manuel Quezon and other leaders of the incipient Commonwealth were filled with foreboding.

One Filipino in ten owes his living to sugar. The growers are concentrated on the island of Negros, which produces about 65 per cent, and in the province of Pampanga on Luzon, producing 25 per cent. The growers are relatively small landholders, grouped about a central depot and mill. The quality of sugar is good, but the yield is low, involving much hand labor. Work is seasonal, and sugar laborers are idle about half the year.

The only crop that rivals sugar in value and sometimes overtakes it is the coconut palm. Filipinos are the world's leading exporters of copra, which is the meat of the coconut. Before independence, the United States took 80 per cent of

Hulling coconuts. The Philippines is the world's largest exporter of copra, or coconut meat.

this crop; in the 1950–60 decade, American purchases averaged 42 per cent. Almost every small farmer grows some coconut palms, especially in the southern islands which are relatively typhoon-free. It is difficult to standardize and upgrade the smallholder's crop and to protect it from a deadly virus known as *cadang-dadang*. It is also difficult to protect the crop from smugglers, who have managed to dissipate the crop as well as the country's revenues. One answer is the coconut plantation, of which there are some excellent examples in the islands. But the smallholder is still the mainstay of this growing source of Philippine wealth.

The third major foreign exchange earner among Philippine crops is a world monopoly. Abaca, sometimes called "Manila hemp," is not hemp but a leaf fiber, the raw material of rope, paper, bags, and other wrappings. Abaca's history involves the strange episode of the Japanese "colony" near Davao on the island of Mindanao. By illegal means, the Japanese acquired 25,000 acres of good abaca land. They imported some of their own labor, and hired Filipinos at two and a half pesos ($1.25) a day, then considered a good wage. By 1939, some 17,000 Japanese constituted an abaca fifth column on Mindanao. It was a thriving colony with its own housing, schools, and a supporting Japanese consulate in Davao. Today abaca is a declining asset, victim of the development of synthetic fibers in industrial nations. It is also a victim of plant diseases and the fact that the average Filipino farmer cannot yet afford the luxury of pesticides.

Sugar, coconuts, and abaca, together with timber, tobacco, and less crucial crops have forged the bonds of economic dependence. They have been exported either raw or semi-

Abaca, or "Manila hemp," comes from the leaves of a type of palm tree. Stripping the leaves is part of the processing.

processed and thus at low prices. At the same time, Filipinos have had to import many essential food and manufactured items at high prices. Trapped in this economic dilemma, the Philippine people came to independence. They have yet to liberate themselves from their dilemma.

POSTWAR

Impoverished after World War II, clearly unable to support itself for many years, the Philippines needed a massive transfusion of American money. It also needed continued free entry of its products, especially of its export crops, into the American market. The new Republic succeeded in getting both, but at the start it had to pay a humiliating price.

The price was exacted by the United States Congress in the so-called Bell Trade Act of 1946. This legislation, named for Representative Jasper Bell of Missouri, its sponsor, provided that free trade between the two countries should continue for eight years—on one condition. The condition was that American businessmen would have "parity," or equal rights with Filipinos, which they had enjoyed under colonial rule. The American Congress repeated its insistence in a second act a few months later. Voting $620 million in war damages to the Philippines, it ruled that no claimant could get more than $500 unless the Philippines granted "parity" to American businesses there.

This condition—nationalists called it an ultimatum—not only conflicted with the Philippine Constitution, but also undercut the independence of the new Republic. The Constitution provided that companies had to be at least 60 per cent owned by Filipinos in order to develop, exploit, and use the timber, minerals, farm crops, and other Philippine resources. The American President had approved this Constitution as a prelude to setting up the Commonwealth. Now Congress appeared to be nullifying one article, and doing so at the moment when the Philippines was presumably becoming a sovereign nation.

Why did the American Congress take what appeared to be a mean and spiteful action? The obvious explanation, pressure from business interests, does not tell the whole story. The 79th Congress, meeting in 1945 and 1946, reflected the national letdown from the high tension and high resolve of the war years. Appeals for help flooded in from half-starved Europe as well as from Asia, from sturdy allies and ex-enemies alike. Never had one country alone been asked to relieve such unprecedented worldwide misery. In the eyes of Americans the Philippines was just one of many deserving claimants. In their own eyes, the Filipinos held first priority, for they had fought and suffered while under American rule. They were not asking, initially, for "aid," but rather for compensation for services bravely performed under the American flag.

Thus the American economic condition was hateful, but the new nation was in no state to resist it. Reluctantly, the Roxas government agreed to amend the Constitution to give American companies the "parity" rights, and Filipino voters approved the change in a plebiscite in 1947.

The United States responded by pouring money into the devastated Philippines. From 1945 to 1949 its aid totaled almost one and a half billion dollars. Apart from paying $400 million for private war damages, the United States gave back-pay to Philippine soldiers, authorized $115 million in those four years for public works, and turned over to the Philippine government mountains of surplus war material worth about $100 million at war's end. Most of the surplus machinery went to work on clearing the rubble and rebuilding; most of the weapons re-equipped the Philippine armed forces. Much of this surplus, unhappily, slipped into the hands of black marketeers and rebels.

By 1950 it became evident that American assistance had not rebuilt the economy. A handful of Filipinos had grown richer, but little of the American money appeared to have seeped downward to the mass of the people. An American commission invited by President Quirino and headed by Daniel W. Bell, Undersecretary of the Treasury, took a long look and produced a scathing report. It indicted the inefficiency and corruption of government, the inadequacy of production, the excess of luxury imports, the failure to collect taxes, the widening gap between rich and poor. It recommended a long list of reforms, amounting to the soundest blueprint ever drawn for a healthy Philippine economy. Among its proposals were a complete overhaul of the tax structure; a planned effort to develop new industries, with incentives for investments; and above all, a long-range plan to lift farm production. The farm plan was more than an exhortation. It proposed the start of community development, the use of foreign technicians, and the creation of rural banks to extend easy credit to poor farmers.

If the Philippine government approved these programs, the Bell Commission proposed that the United States give $250 million in economic aid over five years, in addition to all the other money already committed to rebuild and revive the economy. The Quirino government agreed. A joint Philippine-American economic mission began work in Manila, and "aid," as distinct from compensation, was soon under way.

In addition to American aid, the Philippines received massive help from other sources, public and private. The cumulative total of the foreign aid given had climbed by the end of 1964 to almost $2 billion. More than $437 million of this had come in development loans from financial agencies such as the World Bank and the Export-Import Bank. United Nations agencies had contributed $16 million; regional groups like the Colombo Plan organization, $5 million; and private voluntary agencies and foundations, $56 million. Like other developing countries in Asia and Africa, the Philippines tapped every possible source of help, except two. From the U.S.S.R. and Communist China, nothing was sought or obtained, for the simple reason that the Philippines maintained no diplomatic relations with either. It regarded both as potential enemies.

The former enemy, Japan, contributed not aid but reparations for war injuries. In 1956, five years after the signing of the Japanese peace treaty, Japan and the Philippines finally agreed on $550 million of reparations. Most of this amount, $500 million, was a line of credit for capital goods, a source of supplies which the Philippines had only begun to use by 1965. The other Japanese reparations were $20 million in cash and $30 million in services, such as shipping and training of Filipino technicians and students in Japan.

TARIFFS

In spite of this flow of money from many sources, successive Philippine governments were not satisfied. What rankled especially was the impending threat of tariffs which the American Congress had set for 1954. Wanting to keep free access to the American market as long as possible, the Philippines asked for new negotiations. Thus the two governments in 1954 worked out a compromise known as the Laurel-Langley agreement, named for Philippine Senator José P. Laurel and James M. Langley, a New Hampshire newspaper publisher.

This agreement gave the Philippines preferential tariff treatment in the American market until 1974. It provided that from 1956 to 1958 the Philippines would pay 5 per cent of the regular customs duties; thereafter, the proportion would double every three years, until in 1974 the Philippines would pay the same duties as any other country. At the same time, the agreement let the Philippines speed up the timetable of its own duties on American goods. Imports from the United States would bear a duty of 25 per cent of the regular duties until 1958, 90 per cent in 1965, and the full rate in 1974. The United States thus conceded that its former colony still enjoyed a special relationship. The Philippines, for its part, showed that it had not yet emerged from the economics of dependence.

A decade later, in 1964, Filipino leaders looked with dread to the 1974 cut-off of free trade. They still felt unable to compete with other countries on equal terms in the American market. Demands thus rose in Manila for still another renegotiation of the tariff schedules. Some politicians were tempted to link tariffs to the continuance of American air and naval bases in the Philippines. In other words, if the Americans wanted to keep their bases, they would have to pay for the privilege by giving preference to Philippine goods for a longer time. Up to 1965, President Macapagal had not linked bases and tariffs in this way. But in the nationalistic atmosphere of the mid-1960's, it was probable that the Philippines would try to exact whatever price it could.

The Economics of Development

FOOD

Should an independent nation be able to feed itself? Some, like Japan and Britain do not, and they prosper nonetheless. But the Philippine Islands are blessed with climate and soil, with fields and forests, which could give them great wealth and feed their people generously besides. Why should they not produce this wealth and process it too, thus creating employment and profits?

This is the dream of the new Republic, but the nightmare now has been too little food for the people. To feed itself has, for an agricultural nation, become a matter of pride and common sense.

Almost every Filipino farmer grows some food, and food means rice. The harvest may feed his family, but rarely has he any left over to sell, after paying his share to the landlord and his debt to the moneylender. Although rice grows on 42 per cent of the cultivated lands of the Philippines, production has not kept up with the rising demands of individuals or the needs of the growing population. Almost a third of the mouths to be fed are those of nonproducers of food living in cities and towns. Thus food shortages have become the rule rather than the exception, even though acreage put to rice has multiplied more than five times since the start of the century and yields per acre have increased steadily. However, the yield is still one of the lowest in the world, less than half that of Taiwan, and one-fourth that of Japan. The reasons are not hard to find.

Most farmers in the Philippines use traditional, prescientific methods of growing rice. Upland farms, with about one-fifth of the rice acreage, produce the poorest yields by the crudest means. Each year thousands of hillsides are cleared by the well-known "slash and burn" technique. Seed, neither selected nor washed, is cast over fields, to be watered only by rain. After a couple of years the weeds take over, and the farmer moves on, leaving the hillside to rain and erosion.

Lowland farmers harvest a third more rice by starting it in seedbeds and transplanting it into flooded fields. The low-

land yield could be doubled by irrigation, but this luxury is reserved for less than one lowland acre in three.

Corn is the second most important food crop, and one of growing importance in the Philippine diet. It is cheaper and easier to grow, and more nutritious than rice. But habit prevails. Eight out of ten Filipinos prefer rice and are willing to make the backbreaking effort to raise it. Corn does, nevertheless, feed one-fifth of the people, mainly in the Visayas and northern Mindanao. Like rice, the corn crop suffers from poor seed (hybrid is not yet widely accepted), and a variety of pests. Moreover, corn depletes the soil. It is wearing out and opening to erosion thousands of once-fertile acres on Cebu and other Visayan islands.

The technical problems are not as stubborn as they appear. Robert E. Huke, the economic geographer who has studied them closely, estimates that proper use of fertilizer would immediately increase the rice crop 15 per cent, and pesticides another 15 per cent. The investment would quickly pay off in higher income. But the cost of fertilizer and pesticides is beyond the reach of most farmers.

Even without these, farmers could get better yields if they understood how to select and treat their seed, if they terraced and contoured the fields, if they rotated crops and planted green manures. Even if they accepted these practices, there would remain the need to replace the ancient wooden plow and harrow, the short-handled sickle, or *bolo,* for harvesting, the threshing by *carabao,* and the winnowing by baskets. That so many anachronisms should have survived the 43-year

Some progress has been made in agricultural techniques.
Many barrios *have mills like this one for hulling rice*
that is to be sold on the market.

While rice mills are commonly used for commercial purposes,
many villagers still hull the rice that they consume
by the primitive means of a mortar and pestle. This scene
is in the Sulu Archipelago.

stewardship of the nation with the most advanced agriculture
in the world may seem strange. It was not that American
rulers were blind to the dilapidation of the outdated farm
establishment which they found, or to its resulting hunger
and stagnation. They saw these evils, and they attacked them,
but they failed to uproot the economic institution which
perpetuated them. This institution was the traditional system
of land tenure. Spain found it, strengthened it, and handed it

on to the United States, which bequeathed it almost intact to the Philippine Republic.

THE LAND PROBLEM

Under the prevailing system, the average farm is too small to be economically viable. More than half the farm families work less than five acres of tillable land. More than half hold their land as tenants on large estates. Tenancy, similar to American sharecropping, is older than recorded history in the Philippines. In pre-Spanish centuries, land belonged to the village, and its use was communal. Titles were not known. The village chieftain, or *datu,* gained wealth and authority by assembling as many families as he could to till the village land and to serve him and his family in varying capacities. Thus the free man donated services such as soldiering and house-building but no tribute or crops. The "slave," on the lowest level, was an unpaid farm laborer. Between these two classes, the serf of pre-Spanish days corresponded roughly to the modern tenant farmer; he forfeited half his crop to the chieftain. The serf often fell into dependence through debt, either borrowed or incurred as a fine for some offense. He rarely freed himself from the obligation.

The Spaniards twisted the land system by introducing private ownership of land and by granting large pieces to favored *datus,* Catholic orders, and loyal Spaniards. (See page 66.) As a result, tenancy multiplied. The grants drove many small freeholders off their land or turned them into tenants. At intervals, the Spaniards decreed the issuance of land titles. Again sharecroppers increased, for the rich and powerful knew how to get titles to the best land, while small farmers could not prove ownership. The process has continued. The number of tenant farmers rose steadily from 19 per cent in 1903 to 22 per cent in 1918, to about 35 per cent in 1948, and to over 50 per cent in 1964. During this period landed estates tended to grow larger and landlords tended to move to the towns and cities, leaving hired managers to run their estates.

The villain of the system is not tenancy as such but the conditions that inevitably attach to it. One condition is insecurity. Although the law is supposed to protect the tenant, he cannot protect himself from eviction. He is usually too ignorant and too poor to defend his rights. Another condition is the crop payment which the landlord can exact on pain of eviction. The usual terms leave the tenant little after he has paid half his crop and half the cost of transplanting and harvesting. After that, he must pay on his debt, a third condition. It is not uncommon for him to owe 100 per cent interest on a six-month loan.

Few sharecroppers can get through the crop year without borrowing money and rice to feed their families. Thus the fruits of their labors are already heavily mortgaged in advance to the landlord and the moneylender, who may be the same man. Such conditions make it virtually impossible for the tenant ever to produce a surplus, to save, to make capital improvements, or to move. This, in essence, is his plight.

Nor is it the tenant's plight alone. The farm owner, too, faces insecurity if he lacks a title to his land, or carries a debt that threatens him with bankruptcy and eviction, or does not own enough land to make a decent living. And the business of securing a title can be long, complicated, and full of risk if he cannot furnish proof of ownership.

The tenancy system has produced not only a stagnant rural society but, from the point of view of the landed aristocracy, a stable society. It was far from the American purpose to antagonize the landowners or to disturb their sources of economic and political power. In fact the Americans turned to this leadership group to staff the early experiments in self-government. The first Philippine Assembly of 1907 was largely drawn from members and representatives of the big landowning families. They were the educated, the experienced people, the friendly people, with whom one could deal and get things done both in government and in business. The American regime not only preserved but enhanced their economic position. The only threat to their security was to come later and to grow, as we shall see, out of their very dependence on the United States as a major market.

Even as they strengthened the landlords and their traditional system, the American rulers set about ameliorating the lot of the peasants. They relied upon two instruments: education and legislation. The new generation of Philippine peasants went to school to become better farmers and responsible citizens. (See pages 177–79.) Meanwhile, a series of enlightened laws offered new economic opportunities to them. One set of acts and programs dealt with the opening of public lands and resettlement on them; a second set with the securing of titles; a third, with better terms for the tenant; a fourth, with rural cooperatives and credit facilities. Thus, in 1903, a Public Land Law encouraged landowners to register claims and secure titles. In the same year, Governor Taft arranged for the purchase of the Spanish friars' estates, which were later transferred to 60,000 former tenants. (See page 101.)

When the Public Land Law brought in only a trickle of claimants, most of them wealthy, the American authorities decreed their own survey of land titles. In 1916 a Rural Cooperative Credit Act declared legal war on old farm debt and usury. In 1933, a Rice Tenancy Act specified terms for division of the crop between landlord and tenant. American tutelage of the colony is studded with acts designed to free the peasant from his insecurity and poverty. These acts, however, proved largely ineffective. For one thing, the farmer was slow to take advantage of what they offered him, fearful of tangling with the law and of antagonizing the landlord. Authority had always been stacked against him: a bank was a strange place; a cooperative was outside his experience. His apathy was more than matched by that of the wealthy landowners. They were the educated and experienced people. They could ignore the law or bribe their way out of its enforcement or pay for legal talent to interpret the law to their advantage.

THE NEW LAND CODE

It remained for a few brave political leaders of the Philippine Republic to attack the economic power of the landed aristocracy. President Ramón Magsaysay initiated the first comprehensive land reform law. Its threat to break up the great estates was strong enough to mobilize the vested interests and their representatives in the Philippine Congress. They stripped the law of its effectiveness but nevertheless passed it in 1955. The act served a purpose: it paved the way for a stronger law eight years later. This was the new Land Reform Code, which was finally pushed through under President Macapagal in 1963.

The Code opened with a statement of policy: share tenancy was to be abolished; the tenant was to be transformed step by step into a landed proprietor. First the tenant would become a leasehold farmer, secure on his land and paying a moderate annual rent for it. The new leaseholder would have access to supervised credit at a maximum interest rate of 8 per cent. He would have at his disposal a strengthened extension service and a well-managed cooperative for credit and marketing.

The Code set up a new Land Authority responsible for assembling and acquiring public lands suitable for farming.

Next, it would acquire private lands which had been abandoned or remained idle. Finally, it would acquire from large estates land in excess of 150 acres. All these lands it would distribute on easy terms to leaseholders and landless farmers who showed determination and a capacity to put them to productive use. The big landlord would be compensated, partly in cash, partly in bonds and stocks of a new Land Bank. Large holdings that were efficiently and fully productive would not be disturbed. For farm laborers, the Code decreed a minimum daily wage of about 87 cents, and the right to organize and bargain collectively.

In spite of weakening and complicating exceptions, the law took the Philippine people a long step forward—providing it could be implemented. By 1965, the new agencies designed to carry it out were built and staffed. A corps of enthusiastic young bureaucrats was trained and ready to do the job. What, then, was still needed to get the program underway?

Wolf Ladejinsky, a leading authority on agrarian problems in Asia, has put the onus on the politicians. "It is they who provide the impetus or lack of impetus, who decide between reform and 'reform.' There is no country in Asia," Mr. Ladejinsky has written, "however underdeveloped, which does not know how to write a reform law, or what its implications might be. They have written them, and many have not been carried out—precisely because the political decision-makers understood their implications and their inevitable repercussions. . . . The fact is that national and state legislatures in Asia do not represent the interests of the peasantry."

It is worth noting that the successful agrarian reform programs of Japan and Taiwan were not legislated, but were imposed by authorities, in both cases military, which had an urgent interest in making the reforms work. In Japan they were engineered with the active consent of the peasants, in Taiwan with their tacit consent. Both programs, Mr. Ladejinsky points out, were based on the assumption that the tenant was to gain *at the expense of the landlord.*

If these are necessary conditions for successful agrarian reform, in addition to a good law on the books, then the prospects for action in the Philippines are, to say the least, poor. There has appeared at the top no undisputed authority, political or military, with a vital self-interest in reform. No organized movement of the peasants has developed which might persuade or threaten the authorities or act on its own. And there seems, as yet, no willingness to accept the idea that reform might penalize anyone. In fact, the emphasis has been on a plea that the new code hurts no one and helps everyone. Soon after the law was enacted, Sixto K. Roxas, chairman of the conservative National Economic Council, assured landowners that the new act fully protected their interests and that it had no elements of an "unfinished revolution" (the popular slogan of President Macapagal) or a "class war." Mr. Roxas went so far as to promise the landlords they would become richer by transferring their assets from land into industry.

While the landed aristocrats were being reassured, the cultivators heard the President they had elected describe the new code as an "Act of Emancipation of the toiling farmer from his slavery to debt, poverty, and misery and of his dignification as a human being and as a citizen.

"By this Act of Emancipation," the President concluded, "a new revolution is on." How would the *barrio* people

Mining output increased by one-third between 1956 and 1963. This is an iron ore mine in the Baguio district on Luzon.

respond, if at all, to the dissonant voices of Roxas and Macapagal?

ECONOMIC PROGRESS

From the moment of independence, the Philippine people have been promised a better life by their leaders. This political commitment is being honored, in part. Even without land reform and without a better deal for the tenant farmer, the national economy has grown and flourished in other directions. The effort to modernize and develop got under way in the Quirino administration. It spurted ahead during the Magsaysay period. Even more substantial gains followed in the period from 1956 to 1963.

The national income kept moderately but steadily ahead of the population rise. Mining output increased by one-third; agriculture as a whole by one-fifth; and industrial production by two-fifths. The most spectacular gains were made in the timber industry. The volume of lumber exports almost tripled, while those of plywood multiplied ten times.

Another measure of progress was the growth of new capital in domestic industries. Between 1956 and 1963, investment in new corporations rose from 40 to 200 million pesos; in new partnerships, from 22 to almost 59 million pesos.

These indications of growth, among others, are of interest in their special setting. For the Philippines is one of the newly independent nations seeking to develop itself within the framework of free enterprise. Government is to guide and encourage, but to impose only a minimum of controls. It is to plan and carry out ambitious programs with the aid of a large carrot and a small stick.

Rising investment helped make possible this tin plate factory, the Philippines' first. It opened in 1963.

The carrot consists, in the Philippines, mainly of incentives. These include, for example, a currency uncontrolled since 1963, a system of low direct taxes, and tax exemptions. New industries are stimulated also by government loans and tariff protection. The government does not propose to go into competition with private business. It had one such experiment which proved disastrous, and it does not intend to try another.

What, if any, have been the effects of the growing economy on the lives of the people? For one thing, more goods and more money have not brought serious inflation. The retail price index had risen no more than about 30 per cent in the decade from 1955 to 1965. Wages had increased, but not enough to keep pace with prices. The growth in agriculture had been achieved mainly by putting new land into production. This was made possible by the existence of a frontier area in Mindanao and of pioneers willing to move there.

As for the *barrio* people, what had the political promises of a better life netted them? In 1965, almost twenty years after independence, they had yet to feel the impact of vast injections of money into the economy. Their productivity remained unchanged, which is to say low. Their family incomes had not materially changed. In one respect, however, they had glimpsed the new and better life that had been promised. Soon after independence, a social movement with economic implications began to put down roots in the Philippines. It called itself "Community Development."

SELF-HELP AT THE BARRIO LEVEL

The idea of local initiative was not new. It had found expression in the *barrios* through 4-H work, parent-teacher association, and finally the community school (see pages 179–80). It took President Magsaysay to pull these and other efforts together into an agency called "Presidential Assistant on Community Development." It has been known as PACD ever since. It has trained thousands of men and women to work on *barrio* improvements such as clean wells, fish ponds, feeder roads, and irrigation systems. A private organization, the Philippine Rural Reconstruction Movement, has paralleled PACD's work on a smaller scale. A Yale-educated sociologist, Dr. James Y. C. Yen, decided in 1952 to put his Chinese experience to work in the Philippines, and he gained support for it among well-to-do Filipinos as well as in the United States. Dr. Yen has also concentrated on the training of *barrio* workers as well as on improvement of crops and the creation of credit unions.

There is no precise way to measure the value of the community development movement or to isolate its economic component. Historians of the future may find in it the seeds of a quiet revolution, growing out of the American efforts to educate and legislate, and energized by independence.

ECONOMICS OF "FILIPINO FIRST"

From the strictly economic point of view, a self-imposed handicap to development is the continuing struggle to Philippinize the economy. The fight against "parity," or equal rights for American business, is only one part of the continuous effort to rid the economy of foreign controls. A wider struggle, aimed above all at the Chinese in the Philippines and only secondarily against Americans and other foreigners, is the very heart of Philippine economic nationalism.

Step by step, Philippine governments since independence have moved to shoulder aliens out of dominant positions in import and export trade, retail business, and rice and corn milling. The weapon against alien traders was found in the import and exchange controls set up in 1949. At that time, Filipinos controlled only 23 per cent of their country's import trade. Despite American protests, a law passed in 1950 reserved a progressively larger slice of the import business to "new" importers. A "new" importer had to be a Filipino citizen or a company at least 60 per cent Filipino-owned. By 1957, the Filipinos' share of the import business had jumped to 54 per cent of the nation's total. The Chinese had been dealt a serious blow.

More dramatic was the battle to push the Chinese, and incidentally the Americans, out of retailing. Filipino leaders had been trying to do this ever since the start of the Commonwealth. Earlier attempts were blocked by two Presidents, Osmeña and Quirino. The moment of triumph finally came in 1954, when Congress passed and President Magsaysay reluctantly signed a Retail Trade Nationalization Act. It provided that when an alien—for practical purposes, a Chinese—retailer died, his heirs would have to liquidate the business within six months. If the foreign owners were a company, they would have until 1964 to get out of business or turn their holdings over to Filipinos.

One Chinese retailer, Lao H. Ichong, challenged the law in the courts, on the grounds that it would deprive him of the right to earn his living. He became the Dred Scott of the Philippines, for his lawsuit went all the way to the Supreme Court and led to a historic decision. After two and a half years of delay, the court ruled that Congress had the right to do what it did. Its decision said:

> We hold that the disputed law was enacted to remedy a real, actual threat and danger to national economy posed by alien dominance and control of the retail business . . . that the enactment clearly falls within the scope of the police power of the State . . .

Thus economic nationalism had been proclaimed by the highest court in the land. It became clear to foreign businessmen that the Philippines courts would not support them.

As with many other acts of Congress, the resourceful Chinese found ways to circumvent the law. Filipino dummy owners took over many Chinese retail establishments, and profits continued to flow to the Chinese. As the 1964 date approached for the liquidation of foreign-owned companies engaged in retailing, American businessmen saw trouble ahead. Filling stations owned by American oil companies were classified by the government as retail establishments. New lawsuits were filed, and the issue became one of continuing argument between the Philippines and United States.

As for rice and corn milling, the third field for applying "Filipino First" policies, this hit the Chinese exclusively. A 1960 law gave alien millers three years to get out of business and it set up a 100-million peso fund for a Filipino marketing system. But the law unintentionally hit Filipino farmers. For the Chinese rice or corn miller had also been the moneylender, the source of quick and easy credit for the small farmer. As Chinese went out of business, sometimes moving to the cities and into manufacturing, the Filipino farmer found himself unable to obtain credit except through the cumbersome procedures of the state-operated rural banks. Thus by 1965, the drive against Chinese millers threatened to cut farm production below its already low levels.

In spite of these disadvantages, Filipino nationalists have not slackened their drive. In economic as in political life, they would rather see their country producing less than let foreigners reap profits. Philippine nationalism does not have the chip-on-shoulder stridency of its counterparts in Indonesia, the Middle East, and Africa. In its economic philosophy it remains pro-capitalist and devoted to free enterprise, while most other new nations have socialized their economies. Nevertheless, the Filipino goal is the same as that of other former colonies: to drive out foreign control. This Filipino-first policy is likely to cause international problems.

Social Institutions

Philippine society rests on the family, the school, and the church. These three institutions dominate the lives and engage the loyalties of the people. Each of the institutions has, in its own way, adapted to new political and economic situations, but none of them appears to have been seriously weakened thereby. Two of these social institutions, the school and the church, set Filipinos apart from their Asian neighbors. The public school, to which they send their children, long looked to the United States for its character and philosophy. The church, to which more than eighty per cent belong, looks for its supreme authority to Rome. Only the family pattern links Philippine society to others in Southeast Asia.

The Family

As in rural societies the world over, the family is the framework for social and economic stability. This was true in the Philippines long before the Spanish conquest. The design of the framework has changed comparatively little over the centuries.

A Filipino family unit comprises parents and children, grandparents, uncles, aunts, and cousins on both sides, no matter how far removed. This "extended" family, as it is called, does not live under one roof or in one compound, as does the "joint" family in India, for example. The Filipino family inhabits a number of households, often clustered in one village or urban neighborhood. Each individual household probably shelters a couple of old or dependent relatives.

Four accepted rules have governed and preserved the extended family: authority of the male members; seniority of age; obedience of youth; and collective responsibility.

For a birth, the women of the family assemble; for a funeral, the men. Marriage is an all-family affair, involving formal arrangements between the parents of both parties and a dowry paid by the bridegroom's parents to the bride's. Approval of grandparents must be sought. For engagement and wedding festivities, godparents as well as relatives gather from far and wide.

Among the Christian majority, monogamy is of course the rule; divorce is outlawed. Courtships are heavily chaperoned. Early marriage is frowned on: in the Philippines the average bride is usually over twenty and the bridegroom is older.

The Philippine family has been accurately described as a bank, an insurance agency, and a welfare organization. From the moment a Filipino is born until he dies, his family is his anchor, his rudder, and his refuge. A child soon learns his place in relation to the authority of parents and grandparents; he understands the hierarchy and enjoys the care of brothers and sisters; he accepts childish duties in the home and on the farm. He enters the family business or profession. Home education in traditions, obligations, and skills shapes his life more profoundly than any formal education or friends outside.

The family offers him a job and security in it; it cares for him during illness, oversees his marriage, consults on his own family problems, and deals with them in emergencies. The family cares for him in old age, buries him decently, and tends his grave. Each member receives these services and renders them. In a practical sense, he is part of a rescue squad.

The umbrella of the extended family is further extended by the *compadre,* or godfather, system. Every Christian Filipino is supposed to acquire a godfather at baptism. He is not only the child's guardian, but an auxiliary source of prestige, influence, favors, and last-ditch assistance. He takes his responsibilities seriously.

There are Filipinos who believe that the family structure is crumbling, a victim of migration to the cities, modern education, and a decline in religious observances. Others marvel at the staying power of the family system in what is usually and hastily called this "fast-changing" world. Clearly the Spanish colonial culture fortified the family system, while the American caretakers invaded its domain by assigning some of its private functions to government and by introducing mass education. The shape that education takes in the nationalistic, newly-independent Republic will profoundly affect the future of family life.

Education

The Philippine people came to independence in 1946 equipped with an old and honored system of mass education. Like other parts of the social structure, it was in utter disarray. According to one estimate, three out of four schools lay in ruins. Teachers had been killed or dispersed. The system was rebuilt with miraculous speed, reflecting the value that Filipinos set on education.

By 1950, the new nation of some 19 million people was operating nearly twice as many public elementary schools as before the Japanese invasion and more than twice as many public high schools. In the same period, private high schools had tripled in number, and their attendance had quadrupled.

These accomplishments are a measure not only of the sense of urgency, but of the massive head start with which the people had come to nationhood.

During the rule of Spain, for more than three hundred years, schooling had rested entirely in the hands of the Roman Catholic Church. Where Spain's power did not reach, among the Muslims in Mindanao and Sulu, it had been in the hands of the local *imam* and the mosque. The character of education under both authorities was religious and authoritarian. Children recited and memorized their respective scriptures. Higher education was confined to Manila, where schools and universities were available to the sons of Spaniards and, toward the end of Spain's rule, to a few privileged Filipinos. From these young university-trained Filipinos the independence movement drew some of its outstanding leaders, for example Rizal, Mabini, and Aglipay. Thus Spain, like other colonial rulers, learned the cost of exposing "natives" to higher education.

In 1863, a Spanish decree recognized the responsibility of

the state for mass education. It ordered schools for boys and girls to be established in every community. Spanish was to be the medium of instruction. The intention was remarkable. If it had been carried out, which did not happen, Spain would have done for its subject people what it had never done for its own children at home. While the decree did not succeed, it had set a standard.

When Filipino rebels came, in 1898, to write their own "Malolos Constitution," they declared that "popular education shall be obligatory and free in the schools of the nation." Within two years of this abortive edict, the rebels had gained at least one of their ideals. Even as the United States closed the door to independence, it opened wide the door to mass education. Thirty days after Admiral Dewey sank the Spanish fleet in Manila Bay, a free public elementary school was in session on Corregidor, with an American soldier as teacher.

Two years later, a colony-wide public school system had come off the educational drawing boards of the new administration. It mirrored America's colonial purposes, as Spain's had mirrored its own. The United States had come to "civilize" the islanders, to prepare them to govern themselves. With the school as the main instrument of these purposes, education was secular and democratic. Through the wholly new medium of English, the child plunged into a new world of radical ideas: the dignity of manual labor, health habits, physical training, individual initiative and responsibility. The school reached out to parents, inviting them in for adult education and for service to the school through parent-teacher associations.

American soldiers took off their uniforms not only to teach, but also to help build the first schools. Then, in 1901, a converted cattle ship renamed the *Thomas* landed the

*A Peace Corps teacher, successor to the "Thomasites,"
instructs her young Filipino charges.*

first large contingent of professional teachers from the
United States. Some 540 young men and women stepped into
Philippine history as the "Thomasites" and dispersed
throughout the islands to take charge of city and country
schools. Under vastly different circumstances, but with something of the same spirit, a similar number of Peace Corps
volunteers followed the Thomasites exactly sixty years later.

It was during those sixty years, bounded by the Thomasites
and the Peace Corps, that Philippine education grew into a
massive and indestructible social institution. It leapt from
island to island, from *barrio* to *barrio*. It burst its seams and
nationalized its character. Largely through education, a col-

ony of about 7 million people, without even the skeleton of a public school system or more than an inkling of its value, made itself over into an independent nation of 30 million, equipped with 28,635 public elementary schools, 277 general high schools, 52 agricultural high schools, 47 industrial trade schools, 13 teacher training schools, and 2 state universities—to enumerate only the public schools.

Meanwhile, the American teachers had worked themselves out of their jobs. From a maximum of 1,074 in 1902, their numbers dwindled steadily as Filipino teachers multiplied. By 1940, only 97 Americans remained. In 1960, the public school system was staffed by 105,000 teachers, all Filipinos.

During the same sixty years, three private school systems burgeoned side by side with the public schools. One was the system of Roman Catholic parochial education. Another, operated for profit, was created by private enterprise to meet overwhelming demand. The third was organized by the Chinese communities in an effort to preserve their own language and culture. These schools also were crippled by Japanese occupation and rebuilt after the war.

Filipino authorities have never succeeded in standardizing or controlling their mushrooming school systems. But if Philippine education has seemed at times chaotic, it has never, to its credit, been static. Educators, both American and Filipino, have never stopped evaluating it, overhauling it, and experimenting with it. Changes have, on the whole, been for the better. The early colonial curriculum, for example, made the mistake of transferring Boston or Denver to Cebu or Zamboanga. Children learned that "A" was for apple rather than for abaca, that George Washington was the national hero, and Longfellow the greatest poet. To nationalize the subject matter of the curriculum as well as the language of instruction became a prime purpose of the Commonwealth in 1935. But the war intervened. Today, this purpose is being gradually fulfilled under the Republic.

THE COMMUNITY SCHOOL

One expression of the search for a national identity is the community school, an original experiment begun in 1947. Its declared aim was to serve the whole community by educating out-of-school youth and adults as well as children. The school would train leadership at all levels and thus uplift the community. At the same time, it would enlist the help of community organizations in improving the school.

The idea of using so universally respected an institution as an instrument of social change is just beginning to dawn on educators of newly independent nations. Some decry it as a dilution of child education in the traditional sense. But others argue that it has prepared the ground for community development programs and for democratic self-government in the *barrios,* as provided in the Barrio Council Act of 1963. There is little doubt that the Philippine community school is a beacon and a lasting innovation.

Much remains to be done, however, to upgrade the education system as a whole. In 1960, a thorough survey by a team of distinguished Filipino and American educators brought to light these, among other, deficiencies: First, the system was not serving enough of the children. Of the seven- to twelve-year-olds, more than 12 per cent were not in school. Of the thirteen- to sixteen-year-olds, more than 82 per cent had stopped their education. The law prescribes six years of compulsory schooling; it was simply not being enforced, nor did the facilities to enforce it exist. Fortunately, a seventh year, made mandatory in 1953, was not yet implemented. Not only were truants left at large, but a high dropout rate was

Getting a drink of water in front of school. This is one of the better barrio *schools; most of them are still made of bamboo and palm thatch.*

tolerated. Out of 945,000 children enrolled in the first grade in 1949, only 32 per cent finished the full, compulsory six years. Clearly, the education net was too small; the holes in it were too large. Too many children were growing up to adult illiteracy, either because they had never gone to school or had left too soon. At the same time, talents and skills the country needed desperately were going to waste because of the failure to hold enough children through high school.

Finding the quality as well as the quantity of education inadequate, the survey team reported shortages of teaching materials and textbooks. Although it did not uncover any misuse of public funds, it concluded that "there is not enough money spent to provide good schools for all the children and youth of the nation." This was the judgment, notwithstanding the fact that more than 25 per cent of the national budget has consistently been put into education.

As for the private schools, the report repeated well-known deficiencies. Too many are diploma-mills, admitting unqualified students and handing out degrees to those who had paid their money. Although the government had the power to enforce standards, it had neither the staff nor the budget to do its duty.

THE LANGUAGE BURDEN

Never since the beginnings of formal education have Philippine children been free of a language burden. In a country of at least sixteen major languages and scores of dialects, most children enter the classroom to be taught in a medium they have never heard. So it was for children the Spaniards taught in Castilian, and for those the Americans taught in English. And so it remains. The new Republic has imposed the added burden of a national language called "Pilipino," a simplified version of Tagalog. According to census figures, about 44 per cent of the people speak Tagalog.

National pride demands a national language to displace English, as Hindi is slated to do in India. Therefore Pilipino has been injected into the schools in the following manner: Grades I and II are taught in the local language or dialect. At the same time, children are introduced to Pilipino in Grade I and to English in Grade II. In Grade III the teaching medium switches into English, while Pilipino and the vernacular remain as "auxiliary media." Under this makeshift arrangement, which is probably temporary, Tagalog-speaking children have the advantage of having to learn only one foreign language, not two, in the first two years of school. The addition of Spanish in a later grade imposes a fourfold burden on most youngsters. One result has been a steep decline in the quality of English; yet English is still the main tool from Grade III on. In this situation, the Peace Corps has become a useful although temporary rescue squad. Most of the volunteers have been used as "co-teachers," working not primarily with children, but with teachers, for it is they who need help. Critics of the school system have, without exception, praised the Philippine teaching corps as dedicated, overworked, and underpaid.

HIGHER EDUCATION

In the field of higher education, the Philippines has far outstripped the other countries of Southeast Asia. The new degree mills and the relatively recent obsession with academic degrees among young Filipinos tell only part of the story. Respect for learning is traditional. Among Manila's five major universities stands one of the oldest scholarly institutions in the Far East, Santo Tomas University. This university, founded in 1611 by Spanish Dominicans, has a record of unbroken teaching except during two wars, the Revolution of 1898–99 and World War II. Designed for the sons of ruling Spaniards, it became a training ground for Filipino leaders from the rebel Rizal to President Macapagal.

The university now counts women among its 30,000 students, and admits them to its respected medical school. For scholarship, the Jesuit Ateneo de Manila outranks Santo Tomas, and rivals any institution in the Republic. But in spite of excellence in some departments, Roman Catholic pedagogy no longer dominates the university field. The modern trend is toward secular and vocational learning patterned on the American state universities and land-grant colleges. The University of the Philippines, with 18,000 students at six locations, was chartered in 1906, as part of the grand American design for public education in the colony.

The newest contribution to this design is Mindanao State University. A bold experiment in integrated living and learning, Mindanao State attempts to draw Muslims into the mainstream of higher education. It offers them this opportunity on their own ground. The University opened its doors in 1962, on a 2,500-acre tract of open land. By 1963 it had enrolled 1,138 young men and women, nearly half of them Muslim. In addition to a liberal arts curriculum, plans call for colleges in engineering, fisheries, agriculture, community development, public administration, business administration, and education. The experiment has attracted a faculty of high caliber, including German, Japanese, and American professors. Well over half the students receive scholarship assistance.

Mindanao State sets several useful precedents for Philippine education. It brings together Christians and Muslims on a new basis for understanding. It helps to reverse the tide toward Manila, the overcrowded intellectual center. And it gives the agricultural and mechanical arts another boost toward excellence and respectability.

Religion

Like the family system, religion pervades the daily lives of the Filipinos. The Roman Catholic Church has reported a steadily growing allegiance, which in 1964 it estimated to be 86 per cent of the people. For the vast majority, the Roman Catholic poor, the priest presides over baptism, marriage, and death. The family turns to him in rejoicing and need. Church festivals are almost as numerous as family festivals and often the two coincide. In the *barrios,* where the relationship is most intimate, Philippine tradition and religion have merged into a kind of folk Catholicism.

We have seen how a small band of Spanish friars, arriving in the sixteenth century, converted the Philippines into an

Religion is an important part of Filipino life. Here, a women's meeting in a barrio *church outside of Manila.*

overwhelmingly Christian country, the only one in the Orient. (See pages 60–64.) But for the friars, the Islands might have become an overwhelmingly Muslim nation, like neighboring Indonesia. More than a million Muslims survive to practice their faith in Mindanao and the Sulu islands.

Not until the American conquest was the way paved for the first Protestant missionaries. Some of them ministered, and still do, to the spirit worshipers in the mountainous interiors, people who had fled from the Spaniards and the Muslims. A wide variety of Protestant denominations opened schools, hospitals, and clinics. Their conversions, however, never matched their good works. From the outset, the Protestants took Philippine national feeling into consideration, training a Filipino clergy to work with their own people.

The decline and fall of Spain in the Philippines dealt the Roman Catholic Church there three serious blows. Along with independence, Filipinos had demanded the separation of church and state; this the American conquerors accomplished without delay. Philippine rebels had petitioned Rome to recall the friars. This change the Americans set in motion by buying most of the friars' lands from the church in 1903, and reselling them to Filipinos. Finally, the Church suffered a heresy within its own body in the Philippines.

The Independent Church

One of the first aims of the Philippine rebels was to nationalize the church. When Rome ignored their pleas to replace the Spanish clergy with Filipinos, they denounced the Vatican and established the "Independent Church." Its founder was a Roman Catholic priest named Gregorio Aglipay, who had been a fellow student of José Rizal at Santo Tomas University. Aglipay had no doctrinal dispute with Rome. But he saw the Spanish church and state as twin tyrannies. When he defected, Rome excommunicated him. The Independent Church which he founded in 1902 and headed for many years finally departed from Roman Catholic doctrine. It linked itself first with Unitarianism, later with the Protestant Episcopal Church. The current membership of close to 2 million see their "reformation" as the sole Catholic survivor of the Philippine revolution. They regard Philippine Roman Catholicism today as a relic of colonialism.

Modern Roman Catholicism

In spite of its loss of wealth and established position— some say *because* of this—the Roman Catholic Church in the

Philippines has displayed remarkable survival power. According to its official 1964 report, the church, at that time, operated through 1,680 parishes, maintained 1,337 schools, and taught more than half a million pupils. The church expresses its social concern widely through strong organizations of men, women, youth, and farmers, as well as through the Catholic Welfare Organization.

Rome finally made a major concession to Philippine nationalism: the appointment of a native Cardinal. Otherwise, the clergy remains overwhelmingly of foreign origin. Thus in 1964 there were only 317 Filipino priests out of a total roster of 2,184. Among nuns, however, the balance is reversed, with three Filipinas for every foreigner. As in Spanish days, it is the orders, thirty-one of men and forty-nine of women, which carry the major burden of teaching and healing.

Philippine Women

As wife and mother, the Filipina plays a dominant role in family life. She bears and raises, on the average, seven children. She, more than anyone else, preserves the continuity of family traditions and values. In this sense she is the family's leading educator. She is also the family treasurer, wielding power as she apportions scant resources. Usually, too, she serves as the main link between the family and the church.

As prodigious producers of wealth, Philippine women contribute to the economy of the nation, as well as to the support of the family. More than a million members of the

Many Filipino women acquire technical skills. This girl is a student at the famous Agriculture School of the University of the Philippines.

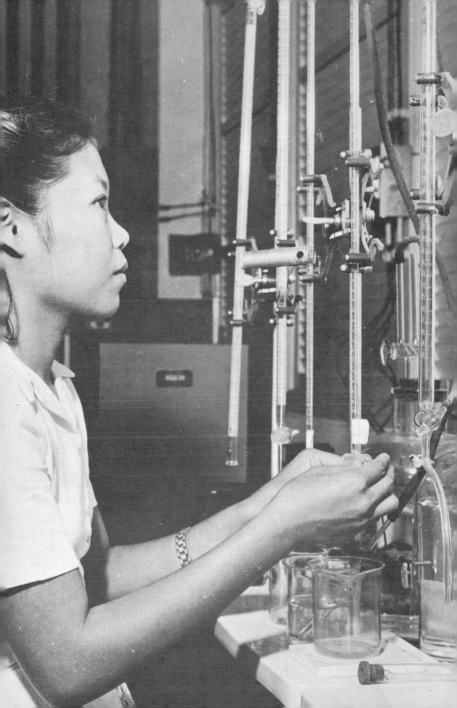

female labor force of three and a half million work regularly on farms. Three out of four of these farm women are unpaid workers, without whose labor in the fields the family could not survive. Anyone who has been in the Philippines during the transplanting of rice seedlings into the flooded fields will appreciate the essential, backbreaking contribution of the Filipina. To this extent, she resembles millions of other women in Southeast Asia. But here the comparison ends.

More than sixty years of educational opportunity have lifted the women of the Philippines out of the conventional Southeast Asian pattern. Their passion for college degrees and for technical skills rivals that of Philippine men, although their opportunities have not. Nevertheless, no fewer than 5 per cent have achieved some college training, a proportion still to be attained by many European, not to mention Asian, countries. A favorite social event among middle-class Filipinas is a reunion of college alumnae between the ages of twenty and sixty.

Philippine women have invaded almost all occupations. In commerce they outnumber men five to three; in industry almost two to one; in teaching, more than two to one. Among women in the professions in 1962, the Department of Labor in Manila reported 18,388 nurses, 14,131 pharmacists (women virtually monopolized this profession), 3,793 dentists, 1,818 certified public accountants, 4,602 physicians, 916 chemists, 497 chemical engineers, 156 architects, 74 civil engineers, 4 electrical engineers, and 1,050 lawyers. A woman justice sits in the Court of Appeals, and three women serve in the Senate. Achievements such as these could not be matched or even approached anywhere else in Southeast Asia. There is no doubt that women are striding ahead all over Asia, especially toward equality under the law. But the Filipina, who gained the vote in 1937, is a pace-setter.

Moreover, there are signs that the educated Filipina is at last beginning to bridge the gap in communication and understanding which has separated her from the *barrio* woman. Girls trained at the Agricultural School at Los Banos are no longer clinging to desks in government departments but are venturing out to teach and demonstrate their skills in the countryside. Even the intellectual cream of the crop, the women lawyers, have organized seminars on civil rights and responsibilities of citizenship for farm women.

Social Welfare

The Philippine family has always looked after its own, thus keeping welfare primarily a private concern. It is estimated that 3,300,000 family units are sheltering and caring for some 4,000,000 additional dependent relatives. With all the generosity and loyalty that these figures imply, the effects have been to spread poverty and debilitate the family as a whole. When the family has failed to cope, it has traditionally turned to the church. Since the earliest days of Spanish rule, Roman Catholic charity has taken the form of orphanages, hospitals, and homes for the aged and infirm.

Public government-supported welfare entered the Philippines with the American occupation, and its first concern was for public health. Americans, in their own interests as well as in the interest of the islanders, introduced mass vaccination against smallpox, inoculation against cholera and plague, and environmental sanitation against malaria and dysentery. In 1925, Governor Leonard Wood sponsored the first large public welfare institution called Welfareville. To the traditional orphanage and home for the aged, it added training schools for wayward boys and girls.

A member of a tribe from the Mountain Province of northern Luzon and an example of his people's woodcarving.

The modern concept of social welfare, with its accent on prevention and rehabilitation rather than on charity, is just beginning to gain widespread acceptance. The first school of professional social work opened in 1950. A Social Welfare Administration was established in 1951. And in 1954 a Social Security Act authorized the first insurance against unemployment, disability, and retirement, providing employer contributions of 3.5 per cent and employee contributions of 2.5 per cent of salaries.

Although minimum wage laws have been on the books since the early Commonwealth days, the legal floor remains at four pesos ($1) a day in urban areas and two pesos ($.50) in rural areas. A broadly based social insurance system assumes the workers' capacity to save out of wages for a rainy day. But because of the low level of pay, most Filipinos still lack that capacity.

Arts and Letters

Filipinos have carried on a triangular love affair with the arts. It has been their fortune, good and bad, to dilute their

Dancers of the world-famous Bayanihan Troupe on their way to a performance.

talents among three cultures. In spite of poverty and malnutrition, Filipinos remain an exuberant people. They love to express themselves extravagantly in their native, pre-Spanish, song, sport, dance, food, and dress. This is the unsophisticated side of the picture. Since independence, national folklore and art have been revived and stylized, made sophisticated and fashionable. One example is the folk ballet, with heavy emphasis on tribal color and ritual. A prime show window of the new artistic nationalism, the Bayanihan ballet troupe, goes on world tours.

A second object of Philippine love has, of course, been Spanish culture. Somehow, the Latin lilt of song and prose evoked a Filipino response. In the late nineteenth century, the affair took on a love-hate aspect, as José Rizal wrote his classic Spanish novels to castigate the culture in whose language he expressed himself so eloquently. This literature of protest and propaganda was, ironically, Spain's outstanding cultural contribution to its colony.

One day in 1898, without notice, Filipinos were asked to take a massive dose of American culture as well. The tendency was, at first, to swallow it whole, and then to regurgitate part of the overdose. It was just another example of the Filipinos' habit of taking what foreign culture they could use, and then rejecting the rest.

Two exceptions come to mind, two instances in which they have kept and digested the overdose. One is American films. Their appeal in the Islands remains universal, even for Grade B and Grade C productions. The more gore and sex in an American film, the more Filipinos flock to see it. The second exception is American popular music, especially jazz. Filipinos have taken to jazz and rock-and-roll as they once took to the romantic ballads and dances of Spain. They have both responded to jazz and mastered it, becoming the most sought-after jazz performers in Southeast Asia.

Europeans sometimes cite the Philippine press as still another example of an American institution swallowed whole. This is not fair to Filipinos; after all, it was one free and hard-hitting newspaper, published by exiles in Europe, which helped to spark their revolution of 1896. But the

Americans did preach press freedom when they came to the Philippines, and the Filipinos took the preachment at more than face value.

Today nothing in Southeast Asia can match the vigor, brashness, and courage of the daily and weekly press in the Philippines. Other newspapers of the region usually cower before their governments, if the governments let them appear at all. In the Philippines no such fear inhibits editors or reporters. Officials from the President down are fair game for attack.

Philippine newspapers pay comparatively little attention to books, art, science, or foreign affairs. They concentrate on politics, crime, and social doings. Most of them belong to families with other business fish to fry, and their news columns as well as editorials reflect the owners' outside interests. The biggest and best of the English-language dailies is *The Manila Times* (circulation 140,000), the only one whose owners have no outside holdings except other publications and broadcasting stations. The true glory of Philippine journalism is not a daily at all; it is the weekly *Philippine Free Press* (circulation 90,000), edited by Teodoro M. Locsin, a fearless crusader for political and economic reform. Few weeklies anywhere can surpass the *Free Press* in the sustained energy and sometimes the brilliance, of its writing.

The Manila English-language dailies alone sell about 350,000 copies a day; the Tagalog dailies, about 70,000; the Chinese, 13,000. This says much for Filipinos' literacy in English and their interest in public questions. The Manila press, with all its faults, is not a stand-pat press. It continually prods its readers by exposing alleged skulduggery in high places. One result is a rash of libel suits, most of which get nowhere. Another is public irreverence toward the holders of political power, whoever they may be.

Surprisingly, the novels, plays, and poems by Rizal's successors have not turned to effective political and social protest. Creative artists in the Philippines do not lack material; it lies all around them, especially the pity and bravery of life in the *barrios*. Yet the twentieth-century Philippines has not yet produced a *Dr. Zhivago,* or an epic of farm life like *Giants in the Earth,* or muckraking fiction like that of Upton Sinclair. Nor have the fine arts so far produced any painters in a class with Rivera and Orozco in that other ex-Spanish country, Mexico. This surely will come.

The Social Structure

On the Southeast Asian landscape, the architecture of Philippine society is familiar: a pyramid rising to a sharp point. Early Filipinos designed it; Spain found it convenient and strengthened it; Americans accepted the existing social order, used it, and trusted in mass education, democratic politics, and time to modify it. The Philippine Republic inherited it virtually intact.

On the pinnacle of the pyramid sit the ruling families. Many of them are direct descendants of the early *datus* and the later *caciques*. Their power has derived first from ownership of large tracts of land and second from the resulting access to wealth and local influence. Spain enhanced their wealth by appointing them tax collectors and enhanced their power by making them responsible for public order. The United States turned to them for leadership in staffing the new institutions of self-government and for captaining new industries. Thus it is no surprise to find in the independent Philippines only about 13,000 owners of more than 150 acres of land, and only 2 per cent of Filipino families accounting for 47 per cent of the national family income.

The modern trend has been for the landed gentry to establish second homes in urban centers, preferably in Manila. There they surround themselves with the latest status symbols: palatial houses, expensive cars, electrical gadgets, and works of art. The move to the city has made it possible to diversify their sources of income with investments in real estate, business, mines, and industry. With added wealth has come the opportunity to send their children to the best schools and universities, both at home and abroad. With wealth and education, fortified by land and local influence, the doors were opened to political power. We have noted how politics appeals to the educated Filipino as a vocation, a game, but above all a means of promoting the interests of the family. (See page 117.) A liberal admixture of Spanish or Chinese blood, or both, seems not to have handicapped them at any step on the ladder. The evolution of the landowning class from local to national power, in a free enterprise economy, has centralized and institutionalized wealth. Nowhere in Southeast Asia are fortunes more secure than in the Philippines.

With few qualifications, the same is true of poverty at the other extreme. On this bottom level, we find 80 per cent of the people. They live by subsistence farming or by menial occupations in city slums. Their common denominator, poverty, is not easy to measure. One could, for example, identify "the poor" as those who earn less than $500 a year per family. But the rural family manages largely without cash, which reduces the income statistic to little meaning. Another way to describe "the poor" is to say that they live without electricity, inside plumbing, telephones, and clean water, and rarely see a car, a radio, a newspaper, or a doctor. But are not these measurements derived from the expectations of a Westerner rather than those of a Filipino farmer?

What is most relevant to poverty in the Philippines is to be found in the farmer's relationship to his land, the terms on which he works it, the methods he uses, and the depth of his indebtedness. These are the circumstances that determine how much a family can produce and earn, how free it is to move, and where it will come to rest on the social pyramid. There is no doubt that the social boundaries have widened over the past fifty years. Whole families have been moving out of *barrios* into small towns, and out of small towns into cities. Although statistics of mobility are not always reliable, it is probably fair to say that the proportion of urban population has grown from about one-third in 1939 to more than 40 per cent in 1965, making the Philippines one of the most urbanized of Far Eastern societies.

Another evidence of the widening of social horizons is the growth of a middle class. In the Philippines, as everywhere in Southeast Asia, the middle of the social structure harbors not one middle class but two: the native and the Chinese.

THE MIDDLE CLASSES

American policies of mass education, free enterprise, and training in self-government encouraged the growth of the middle classes. During the first half of the century, the Chinese community virtually took over the retail and wholesale trades. It provided rice and corn milling as well as banking and transportation services for the Philippine economy. The Chinese educated their children in their own Chinese schools, sent money "home" to China, and surrounded themselves with protective associations, notably the Chinese Chamber of Commerce.

Meanwhile, Filipinos with enough money, education, and family status to exercise a choice were flocking into professions and government jobs. The country came to independence oversupplied with lawyers and well equipped with teachers, doctors, pharmacists, and clerks. There remains a shortage of mechanics, machinists, and technicians in almost all branches of applied science. A middle-class Filipino with a skill usually prefers to live and work in a city, although he is apt to be less stubborn and status-conscious about soiling his hands and serving his rural compatriots than the educated Thai, Malay, or Indonesian.

Since independence, the elite is not as exclusive as it used to be. Some have worked their way up to it by way of wealth, others through politics. Among many examples of the latter one can cite three presidents: Quirino, Magsaysay, and Macapagal. It is not the elite but the middle classes which are likely to be the chief agents of social change in the Philippines. Middle-class Filipinos are still few; one estimate puts their number at 12 per cent of the population. Thus far they have channeled more of their energy into their own personal advancement and that of their families than into social reform. With the farmers still unorganized, there is no social revolution in prospect; and cracks in the social pyramid are more apt to occur near the pinnacle than at the base.

Yet the materials for peaceful, legal change are at hand. To engineer a social and economic revolution, Filipinos have only to implement and enforce the laws already on their books.

The Modern Philippines
and the World

Until World War II, Philippine relations with the modern world had been conducted by and with Spain and later the United States. The Philippines, like other dependent territories in Asia and Africa, had kept closer links to its far away metropolitan power than to its neighbors. When Filipino politicians, editors, and students traveled abroad, their road seldom led to nearby Asia. It led them in the late Spanish days to Madrid, and then, after 1898, almost always to Washington. The colonial system, by its very nature, raised barriers to commercial and cultural contacts and thus to mutual understanding among the peoples of Southeast Asia. Philippine horizons began to widen only on the eve of independence.

The Philippines and the United Nations

It was through the United Nations that the Philippines first stepped onto the stage of the modern world. Although not yet fully independent, not even in control of its Japanese-invaded homeland, the Philippine Commonwealth signed the United Nations Declaration during World War II. Thus it became a charter member of the world organization. The future republic passed one of its most important milestones when its delegates took part in the establishment of the Food and Agriculture Organization at Hot Springs, Virginia, and in writing the United Nations Charter at San Francisco. There the Philippines, in its own right, was helping to build an organization to keep the peace, not only in the Southwest Pacific but around the globe.

From the start, the chief Philippine spokesman, General Carlos P. Romulo, acted as if he spoke for a fully independent nation. At San Francisco, he quickly made himself a leader among the spokesmen of the smaller countries, along with Australia's foreign minister, Herbert V. Evatt, and a few others. By his speeches in committees and in the full conference, by his incessant lobbying and propagandizing behind the scenes, Romulo fought to loosen the grip of the great powers on the Security Council and to enhance the status of the General Assembly. In this he failed, perhaps because the United States stood firmly committed to the Security Council veto. Romulo also fought hard against Britain and other colonial powers to mention the word "independence" in the Charter as a goal for dependent peoples. In this fight he won, with enthusiastic American backing. The Russians, of course, assumed that Romulo was only a marionette, moving and talking as the United States pulled the strings. Joseph Stalin may have been thinking of Romulo's performance when he talked to Harry Hopkins in June 1945. It was a mistake, said Stalin, to believe that just because a nation was small it was necessarily innocent.

At San Francisco the Philippines made the utmost use of its small-power status. Except for five nations from the Middle East, the Philippines was the only small country of Asia represented there. The colonial empires in Southeast Asia had not yet broken up. When Romulo challenged the great powers at San Francisco, he was, in effect, speaking also for the Philippines' neighbors who would soon win their sovereign equality in the world family.

Year after year in UN meetings, the Philippines always kept sight of its small-nation status and of its almost four centuries of colonial history. Again and again Philippine delegates voted for General Assembly resolutions condemning vestiges of colonialism and of racial discrimination. One favorite target for Manila was South Africa with its *apartheid* policy of keeping whites apart from nonwhites. Others were the Netherlands in Indonesia and, later, Portugal in India and Africa. On anti-colonial and antiracist questions in general, the Philippines voted with the U.S.S.R. two-thirds of the time and often against the position taken by the United States.

Yet on cold war issues the Philippines almost invariably stood and voted against the U.S.S.R. and alongside its former American masters. Only once, in 1948, when Communist-supported rebels were fighting to take over Greece, did the Philippine delegation vote against the United States and its European allies on a question of keeping the peace. The Communist invasion of South Korea in 1950 provoked more than a UN vote of condemnation from the Philippines. Four regimental combat teams, totaling about 5,000 Filipino soldiers, were sent to Korea and served under General Douglas

MacArthur's UN command. By the end of 1951 the Philippines had lost fifty killed and almost a hundred wounded. Every vote for the seating of Peking to represent China brought a "no" from the Philippines. Taiwan, with its Nationalist Chinese government, is the Philippines' closest neighbor to the north; no delegation spoke and voted in the UN more consistently than that of the Philippines to oppose any whittling away of Nationalist China's status.

TWO DIRECTIONS

Philippine foreign policy, as shown in the UN, thus appeared to be pulled in opposite directions. In one direction, the delegates from Manila sought to show that their country, too, was new, poor, underdeveloped, and for centuries a colony of Western powers. The Filipinos did this partly because they genuinely loathed colonialism and racial discrimination, partly because they wanted to win new friends among the uncommitted nations of Asia and Africa. In the other direction, the Filipinos always stood as a fully committed anti-Communist nation, fearful of Russia and China and glad to be an ally under Washington's protective shield.

Filipino leaders saw no contradiction in thus seeming to face two ways. In the Philippine view, stated by successive presidents and foreign secretaries, a country can be anti-colonialist without being pro-Communist. The United States did not disapprove. Washington may have believed that the Philippines could be useful as a bridge, a lane of communication, to suspicious and sometimes unfriendly new countries of Asia and Africa.

The Philippines made many attempts, usually unofficially and behind the scenes, to act as such a bridge. In 1949 a Filipino, General Romulo, won the honor of being elected President of the General Assembly. But it was an uphill struggle to win respect for the Philippines. Old suspicions die hard, and the image of the Philippines as an American puppet was kept alive by the Soviet Union and its sympathizers. Twenty years after the San Francisco conference, most Asian and African nations still could not think of the island republic as one of themselves. Who could blame them? Their delegates at the UN met Filipinos who bore Spanish names, who obviously had Spanish as well as Chinese blood, who were Roman Catholic in religion, and who appeared Westernized in all their tastes and manners. Thus the Filipinos remained outsiders among other Asians.

For the Filipino leaders themselves, their country's membership in the UN brought one valuable by-product in addition to other obvious advantages. It gave them their first personal acquaintance with political leaders from all the continents. At San Francisco in 1945, Russian Foreign Minister V. M. Molotov gave the Filipinos a course of instruction in Soviet stubbornness and Soviet tactics in negotiation, a series of lessons the Filipinos never forgot. It was not only the officials of the new Philippine Foreign Office who benefited from such encounters in diplomacy. Successive Philippine presidents followed the American example and appointed leading politicians of both parties to the delegations to the United Nations General Assembly.

Among them were three future Presidents, Carlos García, Diosdado Macapagal, and Ferdinand E. Marcos, a future Vice-President, Emmanuel Pelaez; a Senate floor leader, Arturo Tolentino; and a Speaker of the House, Cornelio Villareal. Usually the Philippine delegation also included the chairmen of the foreign relations committees of the Senate and the House.

In the corridors and the delegates' lounge, these political leaders made their first regular contacts with the Latin Americans, with whom they found much in common; with the Western Europeans and the representatives of the Soviet bloc; and above all, with their fellow Asians. By the mid-1960's, Philippine political life could still be called parochial and inward-looking, but at least its leading figures were men familiar with the leaders, attitudes, and outlooks of the world outside their islands. United Nations sessions were not the only magnets which drew Filipino politicians across the Pacific. The most urgent concerns of Philippine foreign policy from the moment of independence onward involved the United States, not the UN. They were subjects to be dealt with in bilateral talks, not in multinational assemblies or committees. The General Assembly sessions each year gave the Filipino delegates an opportunity to discuss these issues with the United States government through private talks in New York or Washington. The most pressing subjects were the economic points discussed in Chapter VI: claims for war damages, requests for economic aid, and the entry of Philippine products into the American market. The second category of Philippine concerns could be summed up broadly as defense: American naval and air bases, American protection against armed attack, and later, joint or regional action in Southeast Asia to contain Communist expansion.

Bases and Alliances

American and Filipino leaders had long foreseen the need for American naval and air bases in an independent Philippines. Within a month after Pearl Harbor, President Roosevelt promised the Filipino people that the United States would set them free and protect them after the war. He took to the short-wave radio to repeat this pledge in 1943, at one of the darkest moments of World War II. Philippine morale had fallen dangerously. Harsh and hurtful as was the Japanese occupation, Filipinos generally felt the pain of an added wound: the thought that the United States had let them down by failing to stop the Japanese invaders. President Manuel Quezon, the architect of their independence, lay in a Shoreham Hotel bedroom in Washington, wasting away with the tuberculosis that was soon to kill him. Something had to be said to lift Filipino spirits. The President's renewed pledge was his response.

In American eyes, said President Roosevelt, the Philippines already had "the same status as the governments of other independent nations—in fact all the attributes of complete and respected nationhood." Its representatives in exile could regard themselves, and were regarded at the White House, as spokesmen of a country no longer politically dependent. Primarily for this reason, the Philippines was never included in the State Department's planning to set up United Nations trusteeships and strongpoints in dependent areas, such as the Japanese Pacific islands. Bases on Philippine soil would be needed to protect the Philippines in the future, but as Harry Hopkins told the British and the Russians at Teheran late in 1943, they would be American, not international, bases. And they would be set up only by agreement with the Philippine government.

The United States Congress acted even before the end of the war to provide such bases. With the full assent of the dying President Quezon and of his successor, Osmeña, both houses early in 1944 authorized the immediate start of negotiations to keep and add to the American bases in the Islands. In May, 1945, after Quezon and Roosevelt had died, Osmeña and President Truman signed an agreement permitting the United States to lease what bases it needed. As Truman explained afterwards:

> . . . we were anxious that a military agreement with the
> Philippines be concluded in order that we might in the future
> continue to protect them against outside attack. The Filipinos
> themselves were equally anxious to have this protection, be-
> cause without it the republic we were helping to establish
> might sometime find itself helpless.

This was the background. After the liberation and the
subsequent birth of an independent Republic of the Philippines—both of them in fulfillment of American promises—
the United States proceeded to carry out its wartime pledge to
protect as well as rebuild the new nation. The first step was
to turn over mountains of surplus war materiel, originally
worth a billion dollars, as a gift. The surplus jeeps became
transmuted into the gaily-colored "jeepneys" on which Manila based its public transportation. Giant earth-moving ma-
chines now proved themselves essential, not in carving wartime airfields out of the jungle, but in clearing away the
rubble of bombing and shellfire. Of the pyramids of small
arms left behind, tens of thousands of surplus rifles slipped
into the hands of Moro guerrillas in the southern islands or
of Huk insurgents in central Luzon. The remainder served to
rearm and equip the postwar Philippine armed forces.

The next step was to retain the existing bases and to give
them a legal underpinning acceptable to both countries. This
was done in March 1947. Two Philippine-American agreements were signed in that month. The first delimited the
extent, the uses, and the conditions for using bases in the
Philippines. The second provided American military assistance to the Philippine armed forces and set up a joint Military Advisory Group. By coincidence, in the same month the
American President enunciated the so-called Truman Doctrine, pledging help to Greece and Turkey and any other
nation threatened by Communist expansionism. The United
States thus assumed a posture of alertness simultaneously in

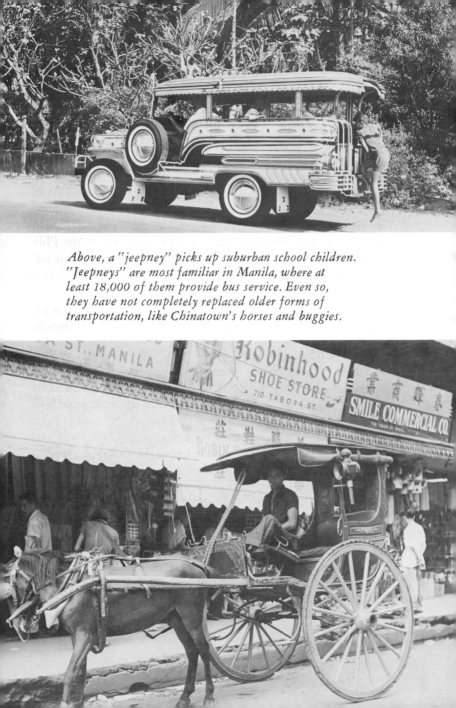

Above, a "jeepney" picks up suburban school children. "Jeepneys" are most familiar in Manila, where at least 18,000 of them provide bus service. Even so, they have not completely replaced older forms of transportation, like Chinatown's horses and buggies.

the Pacific as well as in Europe and the Middle East. This decision marked the start of the worldwide cold war.

The agreement about bases in the Philippines is worth examining closely. It was still in force in 1965, when the cold war had begun to thaw. Probably it did more to shape Philippine-American relations, and thus Philippine foreign relations, than any other action of the postwar era. It gave the United States the right for ninety-nine years to retain nineteen army, navy, air force, and coast guard installations of pre-independence days, and to use seven others if the United States required them because of "military necessity." The nineteen stretched from Batan, the northernmost of the Philippine Islands (not to be confused with the Bataan Peninsula near Manila), to Tawi Tawi in the far south, almost within sight of Borneo.

A few of these bases were small and unimportant, and the United States relinquished them within the ensuing decade. Two, on the other hand, were big and continuously important to the United States in its chain of island bases stretching northward to Okinawa and Japan. These were Clark Field Air Base in Luzon, about fifty-five miles north of Manila, and the Subic Bay Naval Base, about eighty miles northwest of Manila, on the China Sea coast. Clark Field was the place where Japanese bombers caught General Douglas MacArthur's planes on Pearl Harbor day and destroyed them on the ground. Subic had been a naval station in Spanish days. Both were enormously strengthened after 1947. Clark Field became the headquarters of the Thirteenth Air Force; its runways, long enough to take jet planes, were unsurpassed in the Far East; and among its auxiliary buildings, its hospital became the medical center for all Americans, military or civilian, stationed in Asia.

As for Subic Bay, the 1947 Philippine grant included not

only the naval station but the adjacent town of Olongapo, with 70,000 people. The Americans wisely gave up control of Olongapo in 1959 and thus reduced the geographical extent of their base to about that of the District of Columbia. The remainder they developed intensively.

By 1965 Subic Bay bristled with docks and airfields, warehouses and foundries. Here a hundred navy ships anchored every month to be repaired if necessary and to be serviced with everything from ammunition to ice cream for their crews. Here, in underground installations in the surrounding hills, the United States Navy stored enough shells, bombs, torpedoes, and fuel oil to begin fighting World War II in the Pacific all over again. Some 8,000 Filipinos, living in Olongapo, worked on the base day and night under the supervision of a couple of hundred American civilians. The United States, incidentally, paid them 15 per cent more than the prevailing Philippine wage rates; and the ratio of American supervisors to "local" employees was only 3 per cent, the smallest of any American naval base in the world.

Two other installations should be mentioned, for both held symbolic as well as practical value. One was Camp John Hay, a huge leave and recreation center at Baguio, a mile high in the mountains of northern Luzon. To this cool place of enchantment came officers and men of all the American armed services, seeking relief from the debilitating heat of the Asian tropics. Within this compound the streets remained named for American generals and governors, and its golf course and clubhouses kept the atmosphere of colonial rule. The other was the Sangley Point Navy Base, at the entrance to Manila Bay. The United States retained this as a headquarters rather than as a working base, partly for convenience and partly, perhaps, as a reminder that it still controlled the defenses of the Philippines.

BENEFITS FOR THE UNITED STATES

The 1947 agreement gave the United States not only a wide assortment of bases, but also sweeping control over these bits of Philippine territory. Within their limits, and even on their air and sea approaches, the United States gained the right to do virtually anything necessary to operate and control them. Americans could build runways, deepen harbors, and control anchorages and ship channels. They were free to import anything without Philippine customs duties, so long as the goods were needed for the bases and their garrisons. (This included, of course, the cherished American right to set up post exchange shops stocked with American goods.) American servicemen and civilians, and their families, could enter the Philippines freely and stay without paying income tax, again so long as their presence was connected with the bases.

One might have expected the Filipinos, with their love of legalisms and litigation, to hedge these various American rights with all kinds of vexing conditions. But in the 1947 agreements they did nothing of the sort. The new Republic satisfied itself with a general assurance "that the powers granted to it [the United States] will not be used unreasonably, or, unless required by military necessity determined by the two Governments, so as to interfere with the necessary rights of navigation, aviation, communication, or land travel within the territories of the Philippines." It was also agreed, without elaborate conditions, that in applying the American rights outside the bases "there shall be, as the occasion requires, consultation between the two Governments."

The American armed forces could have hoped for nothing better. Although the preamble to the agreement used terms like "mutuality of interest" and "mutual security," Americans held virtually every right except actual sovereignty over the bases. If a Filipino and an American brawled within a base, both could be arrested and perhaps jailed by American authorities. If an American serviceman committed an offense against another American serviceman outside a base, the Philippine police would turn him over to the Americans for punishment. Philippine courts would try servicemen committing offenses against Filipinos outside the bases but would send the Americans to the nearest American base, to be held there pending the trial.

ADVANTAGES TO THE PHILIPPINES

The 1947 agreement on bases stood the test of almost twenty years without renegotiation or substantial change. To the Philippines it served both as a boon and, occasionally, as a nuisance. Its value to the Philippines was obvious. The presence of these air and naval stations on Philippine territory made it unnecessary for the new Republic to maintain a big army, navy, or air force of its own. Were it not for the bases, and for the American guarantee which they embodied, the Philippines would have had to devote a far larger share of its budget to defense. As it was, the country's army in 1965 consisted of only four divisions, of which only one was ready for combat. At the same time the bases made the United States government the largest single employer of Filipino labor. They created jobs, 8,000 at Subic Bay alone, and trained thousands of Filipinos in skills they would not otherwise have mastered.

Such were some of the tangible benefits of the American bases. What about their intangible benefits? Like all intangibles, these were debatable and hard to prove. It may well be that the Filipinos' self-assurance since independence, their lack of a chip-on-shoulder attitude toward outsiders, sprang from their knowledge that the world's strongest military power guarded them. If Moscow or Peking huffed and puffed, Manila did not shiver. One can also suggest—again, of course, without proof—that the American bases enabled successive Philippine governments to maintain civilian supremacy. If the bases had not been there, if the Filipinos had had to worry about their defense and survival, it is conceivable that they might have found it necessary to turn to a military dictator-savior, as other Asian countries had done.

PROBLEMS OF THE AGREEMENT

The existence of the bases, however, undoubtedly embarrassed the Philippines in its relations with the neutralist or nonaligned nations of Asia and Africa. Many of these new countries accepted Communist propaganda which equated foreign bases with foreign control. According to the Communists, foreign bases were vestiges of colonialism and imperialism. How then could the Philippines persuade its nonaligned fellow Asians that it was not an American puppet?

Successive Philippine administrations showed themselves dissatisfied with the 1947 agreement on two main grounds, one affecting the Philippines alone, the other concerning the defense of Southeast Asia.

The first was the sweeping character of American rights and American jurisdiction in and around the bases. In other countries where the United States maintained bases, agreements had been modified during the postwar years and American privileges had been reduced, but not in the Philippines. Why, asked Filipinos, should Japan, the former enemy, get better treatment than the Philippines, the loyal ally? Why should an American sentry, killing an intruder at the edge of a base in Japan, be tried for murder by a Japanese court, while a sentry killing a Filipino in the same circumstances was spared a Filipino trial? Complaints like these echoed loudly in the middle 1950's, most often from leaders of the Nacionalista party.

Conferences about revision of the bases agreements began in 1956, but soon reached a deadlock. American Ambassador Charles E. Bohlen and Filipino Foreign Secretary Felixberto Serrano resumed them without fanfare early in 1959. They agreed, in principle, on several American concessions which would have taken the sting out of Filipino nationalist grievances. One cut the term of the 1947 grant of bases from ninety-nine to twenty-five years; another recognized the Philippines' right to be consulted before ships or planes from the bases could be used elsewhere in Asia; still another required prior Philippine consent before setting up missile sites in the islands. Bohlen and Serrano simply initialed these and other items of agreement, meaning that the issues involved had been settled to the satisfaction of both governments. Other subjects, on which the two governments still disagreed, the negotiators passed over for later discussion. The most vexatious of these was the question of criminal jurisdiction over offenders in and around the bases. In accordance with time-honored diplomatic practice, the initialed items were not to come into force until all the others had been settled and until a complete Philippine-United States agreement had taken shape. The United States sweetened its concessions in October 1959 by turning over a few surplus installations and the entire town of Olongapo, adjoining the Subic Bay base, to Philippine control. It did this without conditions and without waiting for agreement on other issues.

Otherwise, the proposed revisions did not go into effect because the Bohlen-Serrano agreement had been only initialed, not formally signed or ratified. When President García and his Nacionalista party were thrown out of office in the 1961 election, the new President, Macapagal, decided not to raise the issue of the bases again. He preferred to keep the 1947 agreement rather than to make any change that might

impair the bases' effectiveness. But by the end of 1964 grievances had recurred. American sentries shot alleged Filipino intruders, and the old complaints about jurisdiction were revived. Finally, on August 10, 1965, a new agreement removed this irritant from Filipino-American relationships. It gave Philippine courts the right to try all alleged offenders in criminal cases except American servicemen actually carrying out their assigned duties. Thus the Philippines won the same rights extended long ago to Japan and to America's allies in Europe. The agreement on criminal jurisdiction went into effect at once; other changes involving the bases remained to be negotiated.

The second ground for Filipino complaints after 1947—at the opposite end of the scale—was that the grant of bases and military aid did not go far enough to protect the Philippines. In 1951 the government in Manila balked at signing a peace treaty with Japan unless it could get a stronger pledge of military support from the United States. The result was a formal treaty of mutual defense, which took effect in August, 1952. Still Manila was not satisfied. The treaty provided only for consultation in the event of attack. This, in the Filipino view, was not an ironclad pledge; nor was the treaty provision that each party would "act to meet the common danger in accordance with its constitutional processes."

The SEATO Alliance

Philippine and American anxieties deepened as the Communists tightened their hold on mainland China and as Com-

A demonstration early in 1965 against the shooting of trespassers at United States bases. An agreement giving Filipino courts jurisdiction over criminal offenses helped remove some of the irritation.

munist-led forces threatened to seize control of Vietnam and Laos. By 1954 the United States was more willing than before to give an ironclad guarantee—if the Philippines and other countries could be enlisted in an alliance to defend Southeast Asia. Manila was chosen as the place where, in the autumn of 1954, eight nations established the Southeast Asia Treaty Organization, with headquarters at Bangkok, capital of Thailand..

The eight were the United States, Britain, France, Australia, New Zealand, and only three Asian countries: the Philippines, Thailand, and Pakistan. Each signer recognized that "aggression by means of armed attack in the treaty area against any of the Parties, or against any State or territory which the Parties by unanimous agreement may hereafter designate, would endanger its own peace and safety. . . ." This was a weaker paraphrase of the statement in the North Atlantic Treaty of 1949 that an armed attack against one or more of the signers, in Europe or North America, "shall be considered an attack against them all." The Philippine Senate ratified the treaty by 18 to 0, with two abstentions. The new Republic, only eight years old, was now a full-fledged military ally of the United States.

The weaknesses of SEATO soon became as apparent to the Philippines as to its other members. The danger in Southeast Asia was less a threat of outright invasion, like that in Korea in 1950, than of subversion from within. Filipino delegates tried hard at subsequent SEATO meetings to shore up Southeast Asia in two ways. The first was to use SEATO as a channel for vast new economic aid, presumably from the United States. In this attempt the Filipinos failed. The second was to use the collective experience and knowledge of the SEATO members to prevent subversion and to fight it. In this they won some success. The Philippines, after all, had gained precious experience in its successful struggle against the Huks. It now pooled its knowledge with that of its treaty partners and continued to advise and help the SEATO organization, at its Bangkok headquarters, to plan "counterinsurgency" on the Southeast Asian mainland.

In the years following the conclusion of the SEATO treaty, official Philippine interest turned increasingly toward regional cooperation in Southeast Asia. Geographically, Southeast Asia forms a well-defined region; ethnically, many of its peoples are related; politically, all except the Thais had experienced the bitterness of colonial rule. What could be more natural, then, than for all of them to cooperate? The hollowness of this assumption soon became apparent. The Philippines involved itself in a territorial and political dispute which proved that Southeast Asia was not yet a region in spirit, whatever the theorists might say.

The Borneo Dispute

If a Westerner in the 1950's had listed the Asian areas where a crisis might explode in the next decade, his least likely choice would have been North Borneo. Nothing serious ever seemed to happen in this British colony—nothing, that is, except a brutal Japanese invasion and occupation in World War II. Britain had controlled it since the early 1880's, first through a private chartered company and then, after Japan's surrender, as a crown colony.

North Borneo was neither very rich nor very poor. Its forests supplied valuable hardwoods; its mangrove trees provided a product called kutch, important for the tanning of leather; its caves on the eastern coast yielded birds' nests that were treasured for making Chinese soups in Hongkong. In a territory about the size of South Carolina, its sparsely settled population—437,000 in 1959, including minorities related to the Muslims of Mindanao—lived together in peace and apparent contentment. Well might the British governors pride themselves on the law and order in their colony. While international gales blew elsewhere in Southeast Asia, North Borneo remained seemingly safe and untroubled.

To some Filipinos, however, North Borneo did not deserve its immunity. One of these Filipinos in the late 1940's was a young second secretary in the Philippine embassy in Washington. His name was Diosdado Macapagal. Digging into the modern history of Borneo, Macapagal concluded that the British had no right to be there at all. The eastern part of the territory had been claimed, if not controlled, by the Sultan of Sulu, one of those Moro leaders in the southern Philippines who had long resisted Spanish and every other foreign rule. The British held North Borneo because an agent of British businessmen had made a deal with the Sultan in 1875. In return for guns, the Sultan gave him the right to develop North Borneo for an annual fee of 5,000 Straits dollars.

Translating from the Arabic in which the contract with the Sultan had been written into English, the British assumed that he had agreed "to cede." The Sultan and his heirs, and young Macapagal in Washington, insisted that the verb really meant "to lease." According to this interpretation, the British in North Borneo were little better than squatters.

Filipino lawyers in and out of the government were quick to scent an opportunity here. Had not the Sultan of Sulu acknowledged American authority in 1902? And had not the United States then turned over all of its authority in the Philippines to the independent republic in 1946? So, the legalists in Manila argued, the Sultan's lands in Borneo belonged not to Britain, but to the Philippines. The irony of this reasoning seems not to have occurred to its authors. The Philippine government had shown little concern or sympathy for the Muslim chiefs in its own southern islands. Manila had never succeeded in winning universal respect or obedience there; the proof was incessant piracy, smuggling, and banditry in the Sulu islands. Yet Manila now dusted off a contract made by a Sulu chieftain almost a hundred years before and used it as the basis for a national territorial claim.

As long as Britain governed its Borneo colony, the Philippine government had not advanced the claim officially. Why should it now want North Borneo? Why should the new Republic risk an international quarrel to obtain it? Only an expert on the complexities of human behavior could answer these questions. The Philippines did not need land. Nor did it need North Bornean products which competed with its own. Its Muslim citizens in the southern islands did not want to live and settle in North Borneo; they wanted only to travel back and forth, no doubt to get supplies for smuggling, and to keep up personal and religious ties with some of the Borneans living along the coast.

Suddenly, late in 1961, Filipino hesitations ended. The British, with unexplained haste, decided to turn over their bits and pieces of colonial real estate in Borneo—namely, Sarawak and Sabah (the new name for North Borneo)—to a new federation of Malaya and Singapore. They consulted neither the Philippines, within sight of the Borneo coast, nor Indonesia, whose territory bordered that of the British colonies for almost a thousand miles. Early in 1962 Macapagal, by that time President, officially claimed the eastern part of North Borneo for the Philippines—the same Macapagal who, as a young diplomat, had found British possession of the territory built on empty air.

The British rejected the claim. They did not take it seriously. They assumed that the Filipinos were simply using it as blackmail to obtain a large cash payment. Such a proposal was, in fact, made to the Prime Minister of Malaya, the

Tengku Abdul Rahman, by a private Filipino promoter and indignantly rejected. In London the British behaved with offhand rudeness toward a Filipino delegation headed by Vice-President Emmanuel Pelaez. Now Filipino pride was affronted—and more than pride.

The Philippines pressed its claim on political as well as on legal grounds. Now its spokesmen talked also about the Chinese living in Singapore, and of Communist China's designs on Southeast Asia. More than a million Chinese, many of them leftist and even Communist, already dominated Singapore's political and commercial life. If Singapore now joined the Borneo colonies in a new federation, so Filipino officials asked, what could stop a flood of Chinese from pouring into the relatively empty North Borneo lands? What could prevent the emergence of a dangerous Chinese-dominated regime in Borneo, at the Philippines' back door? In this fear, and in a generally anti-Malaysia position, the Philippines joined its giant neighbor to the south, Indonesia. The Indonesians had reason to be violently aggrieved at the incorporation of the Borneo colonies into Malaysia, and they took violent action. Blasts from the powerful Indonesian Communist party denounced the proposed federation as "neo-colonialism." Late in 1962 Indonesia covertly backed an armed rebellion in the British protectorate of Brunei on Borneo's west coast; the leader of the revolt fled to Manila, as if to show that the Philippines supported him. As plans for the new federation took shape, both the Philippines and Indonesia drew together to block it if they could.

Their flirtation culminated in a Manila conference in July, 1963. Officially there were three main participants: President Macapagal of the Philippines, President Sukarno of Indonesia, and Prime Minister Abdul Rahman of Malaya. (At that time the federation of "Malaysia" had not yet been formed.) Actually Sukarno dominated the proceedings, inside and outside the conference room. Using every artifice of showmanship, he flattered the Filipinos and at the same time sought to impress them with Indonesia's power. Students at the University of the Philippines, at a mass meeting, heard him boast of Indonesia's armaments, jeer at Western influence, and defy the "colonialists." They applauded him until the palms of their hands were sore.

The conference took two main decisions, both designed to stave off the formation of Malaysia. The first was an attempt to create a new economic and cultural alliance of the three nations, which are largely of Malay stock. The name they gave this alliance, Maphilindo, was as artificial as the concept itself; it was formed, of course, from portions of the names of the three member countries. The Philippine reasoning behind it will be discussed later in this chapter; here only its relevance to the Borneo dispute needs to be mentioned. Maphilindo was a last-minute effort to draw Malaya away from Britain, and so kill the British-approved plan to absorb the Borneo colonies.

The second decision taken in Manila led to the dispatch of a United Nations mission to Borneo to ascertain whether the people there really wanted to join Malaya and Singapore. By this device, the Philippines and Indonesia succeeded in delaying the formation of Malaysia—but only, as it turned out, by seventeen days. The British put obstacles in the way of Filipino and Indonesian "observers" sent to watch the UN emissaries. When each government asked for the admission of five "observers," British suspicions were aroused. The British had no intention of admitting spies and propagandists to Borneo in the guise of diplomatic opinion-pollers. They denied entry visas to all except two for each country, and delayed the visas for the rest. When the "observers" finally arrived, British colonial officials kept them under careful watch. The United Nations group reported that the people did, in fact, favor the union. Without waiting for the publication of their full report, Prime Minister Rahman announced the formation of Malaysia on September 16, 1963.

At this moment the structure of Maphilindo fell apart. Both the Philippines and Indonesia refused to recognize the new federation and withdrew their diplomatic representatives from Malaya. The Malayans reciprocated. Indonesia went much further. To the accompaniment of loud propaganda, it proclaimed a policy of hostile confrontation and launched a campaign of boycotts and bullets to "crush Malaysia." Before long, Indonesian-led guerrillas, including regular army units, crossed the jungle borders into the former British colonies. And the Filipinos found themselves with a jungle war sputtering at their southern back door.

At this point President Macapagal and his advisers sought to act as honest brokers between Indonesia and Malaysia rather than as protagonists. Trying to effect a cease-fire, they again invited President Sukarno to Manila. This time, in January 1964, both Filipino officials and people were cool toward him. On the day he arrived, he showed discourtesy by keeping President Macapagal and other dignitaries waiting two and a half hours at the airport in the middle of a broiling day. When he placed a wreath on the Rizal monument one sunny morning, his gesture was well publicized in advance, but less than a score of Filipinos bothered to come off the streets to watch him. Anti-Western students still agitated against the American bases and the Seventh Fleet, but somehow Sukarno had ceased to personify their grudges. Politically conscious Filipinos, students and elders alike, seemed not only disenchanted but bored with Sukarno. The Philippine government now worried about Indonesia. The burning of the British Embassy in Djakarta, the sacking of

British homes, the dropping of paratroops on the Malayan mainland, Indonesian propaganda against the American Seventh Fleet based in the Philippines, the growing power of the Indonesian Communists—all these developments produced second thoughts in Manila. The Philippines did not abandon its claim to North Borneo, but wished fervently that it could be brought before the World Court and there put on ice during a few years of adjudication.

Looking across these narrow seas, Filipinos drew no comfort in 1965 from the breakup of Malaysia. Leftist Singapore now stood on its own as an independent state; the Borneo territories might want to do the same. If these weak and underpopulated former colonies also broke with Malaya, they might become even more tempting to pro-Communist Indonesians and to pro-Communist Singapore Chinese. As seen from the Philippines at the end of 1965, Southeast Asia was dark and full of danger.

More worrisome to the Filipinos than any other Indonesian action was the rumored infiltration of Indonesians into Mindanao. Could it be that Sukarno was trying to intimidate the Philippines? Could he be planning guerrilla action there, too? The possibility of defection and detachment by the Muslims in the southern islands had always given nightmares to the authorities in Manila. When President Macapagal paid a state visit to Washington in October 1964, he asked for American help in setting up a new base for the Philippine armed forces in Mindanao, directly across narrow seas from Indonesian territory.

Prospects of Regional Cooperation

Throughout this book we have emphasized the Asian components of the Filipinos' life and character. The Philippine people are overwhelmingly of Asian stock, with a slight admixture of European; their ancient culture came straight from the great civilizations of Asia; their pre-European languages had Sanskrit.origins; their commercial and other contacts were Asian; and their rural way of life can hardly be distinguished from that on the other side of the China Sea on the Asian mainland. At the same time, the Filipinos bear the intellectual and religious imprint of two Western powers, Spain and the United States. Their new republic remains dependent, economically and militarily, on the United States, and their leaders choose to be American in their tastes, their attitudes, and to some extent in their way of life.

Is it any wonder that such a nation, pulled one way by Asia and another by America, should suffer from a split personality? It would not be fair to call this condition schizophrenia, for the Filipinos are the least neurotic of the Asian peoples. Nevertheless, their Republic remains difficult to classify, in the opinion of Asians and Americans alike. It is undervalued by many Asians, as a Christian and somehow un-Asian country off their shores, and equally undervalued, as well as taken for granted, by many Americans as a semi-dependency which will always have to do Washington's bidding. In no aspect of the life of the Philippine Republic is this constant pull and counter-pull more apparent and more damaging than in its official relations with other countries.

During the Republic's first eight years, the work of physical reconstruction and nation-building took priority over foreign relations—except, of course, for relations with the United States. Filipino leaders, with a few articulate exceptions, had little time or inclination for creating a Philippine "image" abroad. By 1954 these priorities began to change. A few perceptive Filipinos came to see that their nation was virtually an outcast among Asians. Successive Presidents consciously tried to show that the Philippines was not at all a

Westernized republic planted off the shores of Asia, and not merely a satellite of the United States.

One example of this effort was the changing of Philippine Independence Day from July 4, the independence day of the United States, to June 12, the anniversary of Aguinaldo's proclamation of a free republic in 1898. Another example was a deliberate change in the habit developed by Philippine leaders of frequently making official or unofficial visits to Washington. Instead, President Carlos P. García paid state visits to Vietnam, Cambodia, and Laos. Then his successor, President Macapagal, made a series of ceremonial visits: first to Madrid, Rome, and Karachi; then to Tanganyika, and to the Malagasy Republic in Africa, a new nation with people of part-Malay stock who speak a Malay-related language; and finally, to Cambodia and Indonesia. On all these journeys, the Filipino leaders proclaimed their concern for developing peoples who were humiliated and held back like the Filipinos themselves by colonial masters.

During the 1950's one concept took precedence over all others—the concept of regional solidarity among the peoples of non-Communist Asia. An early and premature example of its application came in 1950, when President Quirino invited representatives of Australia, Ceylon, India, Indonesia, Pakistan, the Philippines, and Thailand to meet at Baguio. A group of such diverse nations could hardly be expected to agree on any policy. Their representatives merely signed a declaration calling for social and cultural cooperation and for raising the economic standards of underdeveloped peoples.

This was little more than talk. Another example of talk—but effective talk—was provided by the Bandung Conference of Asian and African countries in 1955. Here the Philippine delegation spoke out boldly against communism, in the presence of Foreign Minister Chou En-lai of Communist

China. It also paid special attention to the delegates of Southeast Asia and India, whether committed or "non-aligned."

Year by year, particularly after the start of the Macapagal administration in 1961, more Filipinos found hope in the dream of a regional association of Southeast Asia. If such a grouping could become a reality, they believed, it would serve Filipino interests in at least three respects. It would check Communist China's power to intimidate small Asian countries, one by one. It would symbolize the lessening of Philippine dependence upon the United States. And it would give Asia a badly needed new "image" of the Philippines.

Frequent discouragements and setbacks did not stop the Philippine thinkers and phrase-makers. They remained committed to Maphilindo and to what President Macapagal called "our regional integrity in Asia." Speaking in Manila on January 9, 1964, to a Rotary Club audience which included many Americans, he said:

> We shall manifest this commitment [to regionalism] by accepting the undeniable fact of our geography; by never deviating from the inescapable truth that we are in and of Asia. We shall pursue this commitment without in any way reflecting on the policies and aims of other societies of the different nations within our region.
>
> Cultural and educational exchanges between our Republic and the other nations of Asia shall be encouraged; closer and cordial consultations on matters affecting the security of the region shall be promoted; and schemes that will enhance the understanding of our people about the humanity and cultures of other Asian countries shall be deemed good and proper . . .

If the aim was one of "widening our intellectual horizons," as Macapagal put it, Philippine schools and colleges could do much to achieve it. But if the President seriously believed he could create a regional spirit and a regional grouping in Southeast Asia, he was even more of a dreamer than his conservative political enemies contended. In spite of geography and heritage, Southeast Asia stubbornly refused to behave like a region. Neighbor assailed neighbor and sometimes shot at him. A bad-neighbor policy was the only region-wide policy at work. One might as well have talked of regional cooperation in the Balkans before 1914 as in the quarrelsome, fragmented Southeast Asia of 1964. President Macapagal was describing a hope, not a reality, when he said that year: "It has become possible now . . . to conceive of regional defense and national security not necessarily dependent on any of the big powers but at the same time continuing close relations of goodwill and friendship with them." Whatever the hope, its realization, he conceded, was not "possible now." With two formidable powers, the Soviet Union and China, the Philippines still had no diplomatic or private relations. Its security depended on one power alone: the United States.

Security versus Identity

The reality of Philippine foreign policy, as distinct from the dream, involved chiefly Indonesia, China, and the United States. On Indonesia and its volatile President Sukarno, many Filipino nationalists looked with the indulgence an adult shows toward a teen-ager. Official Philippine policy continually made allowances for Indonesian actions. Its policy was to maintain contact with Indonesian leaders and not to let Indonesia become isolated. "If you will look up our President Quezon's speeches about 1916," one Philippine leader told the authors, "you will find them just as excitable as President Sukarno's now." But there was a difference, and Filipino officials were aware of it. Indonesia had a population of more than 100 million. Moscow-supplied armaments gave it the strongest army, navy, and air force in Southeast Asia. It is a Muslim country, closely linked by religion and geography to the southernmost Philippine islands. And it has the strongest Communist party in Southeast Asia, a party which has nothing but contempt for the rich *mestizos* who, in its opinion, lead the Philippines. Too close an embrace with such a neighbor could be suffocating and deadly. Thus the Philippines looked ahead with anxiety to the struggle for power which, its leaders believed, would inevitably follow the passing of President Sukarno from the Indonesian scene. In the mid-1960's Manila began to be preoccupied with staving off Indonesian penetration—commercial, propagandist, and perhaps subversive—into the southern part of the Philippine Islands.

Meanwhile, Filipino leaders looked with deepening concern on Communist China. What troubled them was not only the growing prestige of the Mao Tse-tung regime on the Southeast Asian mainland. Manila's anxiety was caused by the Chinese who live in the Philippines, variously estimated at from 300,000 to 500,000. What, they asked, would happen if Peking succeeded in establishing subservient regimes from Burma to South Vietnam, and even in Singapore? What would be the effect on the Chinese in the Philippines? Leaders in Manila said repeatedly that they would not recognize the Peking government, even if the United States did so. They do not want a Communist Chinese ambassador in Manila to serve as a kind of commissar over the Chinese throughout the Philippines. No doubt the Philippines could maintain a policy of nonrecognition; after all, former Malaya (now Malaysia) did not recognize either the Communist Chinese regime on the mainland or the Nationalist Chinese regime on Taiwan, and yet traded from time to time with both. But if Southeast Asia were ever dominated by Communist China, the Philippine dream of regional cooperation would evaporate. And then the Republic would face a painful choice: either to establish relations with Communist China or to become dependent upon the United States.

Are these the only alternatives? Filipinos sometimes consider a third possibility, neutralism. This course, which would involve a break with the American connection, was advocated for years by the late Senator Claro M. Recto, a brilliant, patriotic, but erratic constitutional lawyer. Among Recto's disciples, particularly in academic circles, are some who think the Philippines would have been spared the blood, tears, and destruction of the Japanese invasion if it could have been neutral in 1941. Neutralism implies an end of the mutual security treaty with the United States, as well as the ultimate withdrawal of Americans from their Philippine bases.

Since Senator Recto's death, not one nationally important Filipino leader has advocated abandonment of the connection with the United States. But dependence on another country is always galling. As we have seen, irritation over the military bases has erupted again and again. The real cause of the trouble is a sense of frustration on the part of Filipinos because of their dependence on a foreign country, even one as friendly and as much admired as the United States. Thus neutralism and nationalism are linked in the Philippines as elsewhere in Asia. And every Filipino politician must be a nationalist if he is to remain in power. Given these circumstances, the overriding task of Philippine foreign policy in the mid-1960's was somehow to reduce the country's sense of dependence on Washington without making the Republic vulnerable to Communist or other dangers.

This book, as its title makes clear, deals only with the Philippines "yesterday and today." To foretell the future of the Republic, or of its foreign relations, is not its purpose. But this much can be said: the Philippines can never be either wholly Asian or wholly Western. No Asian country that has been ruled by Westerners for centuries can stamp out all Western influence—or would wish to—the Philippines least of all. To do so, Filipinos of future generations would have to abandon their Catholic religion, their use of the English language, their Spanish surnames, their partly American politics, their many Western tastes and aspirations. At the same time, Filipinos cannot escape from their Asian geography or ethnic origins, or from their Asian cultural heritage.

Thus the Philippines will continue to be something of a hybrid in its foreign relations. It cannot feel comfortable either as a member of an Asian anti-Western bloc or as a Western outpost, a kind of Hawaii off the Asian mainland. It will have to maintain close ties with the United States and at the same time it must constantly cultivate its ties with its Asian neighbors. It will have to seek the best from both worlds.

Glossary

abaca (ah-bah-*kah*)—a leaf fiber, sometimes called Manila hemp, used for rope, bags, and other wrappings; an important export.

Audiencia (ow-*dyen*-thia)—the highest court of justice in the Spanish administration of the Philippines and other colonies, often used to advise the governor-general and the king.

barangay (bah-rahn-*gye*)—a large Filipino village or group of small villages, usually of from thirty to a hundred families, in pre-Spanish and Spanish days.

barrio (*bah*-ree-oh)—a Filipino village, or a rural subdivision of a municipality.

barrio lieutenant—the headman of a Filipino village, formerly appointed, now elected.

bolo (*boh*-loh)—a multipurpose knife, usually curved and single-edged, used as a weapon and farm implement.

cacique (ka-*seek*)—a word imported by the Spaniards from the West Indies, meaning in the Spanish Philippines chieftain of a *barangay* or group of *barangays;* in present times, a person of commanding local influence, or a political boss.

carabao (kah-rah-*bah*-o)—a water buffalo; the indispensable beast of burden in the rural Philippines.

Cebuano (say-*bwahn*-o)—a native of the island of Cebu; also, a widespread dialect spoken in Cebu and other Visayan islands.

Commonwealth—the form of Philippine government set up in 1935 as a transition to full independence.

compadre (kawn-*pah*-dreh)—a godfather; in Spanish America and the Philippines, one who extends friendship and protection.

coolie—an unskilled city laborer, such as a porter or stevedore. The term is usually applied to Chinese laborers by Filipinos and Westerners.

copra (*kop*-ra, *kohp*-ra)—dried coconut meat, used chiefly for coconut oil: an important Philippine export crop.

datu (*dah*-too) or **dato**—the traditional village or tribal chieftain, forerunner of the *cacique*. The term survives only among Philippine Moslems.

encomienda (en-koh-*myen*-da)—in the early Spanish days, a feudal grant entitling the owner to take tribute from the people on his land and requiring him to protect them. The colonial administration awarded such grants to loyal *datus,* Catholic orders, Spanish military officers, and others.

galleon (*gal*-ee-un)—a large sailing ship used by the Spaniards in the sixteenth, seventeenth, and eighteenth centuries to carry rich Oriental cargoes from Manila to Mexico.

garrote (gar-*roht*)—a Spanish mechanism for executing by strangulation, usually with an iron or wooden collar tightened around a victim's neck by a winch or handscrew.

Huks (hooks)—abbreviation for **Hukbalahaps** (hook-bah-lah-*hops*), members of a Philippine guerrilla movement which became Communist-dominated and was outlawed in the late 1940's.

Ilocano (ee-loh-*kahn*-o)—a native of the two Ilocos provinces on the northwest coast of Luzon; also, the dialect widespread in and around that area.

imam (ee-*mahm*)—among Moslem communities in the Philippines, the man who conducts services in a mosque.

jeepney (*jeep*-nee)—a Filipino adaptation of the small American vehicle with four-wheeled drive, the jeep: used as a passenger bus in Manila and other cities.

junk—a Chinese sailing ship used in coastal waters and narrow seas for carrying cargo and, sometimes, passengers.

Katipunan (kah-tee-poo-*nahn*)—a secret revolutionary society formed in 1892 to free the Philippines from Spain.

Kempitei (kem-pee-tay)—the secret police of the Japanese occupying forces in Asian countries during World War II.

kutch, or **cutch**—an extract of the bark of mangrove trees, used for tanning leather.

Malacañang (mah-lah-kahn-*yahng*)—the official residence of Philippine presidents, on the Pasig River in Manila; formerly the home of Spanish and American governors-general.

Malay (muh-*lay*)—a member of an ethnic group, sometimes called the brown race, the dominant strain in the Philippines, Indonesia, and the Malay Peninsula.

Malaya (muh-*lay*-a)—the former federation of states on the Malay Peninsula which became independent, within the British Commonwealth, in 1957; merged in 1963 into the larger Malaysia.

Malaysia (muh-*lay*-zia)—a federal kingdom made up of Malaya, Sarawak, and Sabah (formerly North Borneo).

mangrove—a tropical tree or shrub that grows in swamps, common along the coasts of Borneo and the southern Philippines.

mestizo (mes-*tee*-zo)—in the Philippines, a person of mixed Filipino and foreign ancestry.

monsoon (mon-*soon*)—in the tropics and subtropics of Asia, a seasonal wind from the ocean which brings heavy rain.

Moro—the Spanish name for the Moslems of the southern Philippines; copied from the name of the Moors who conquered Spain.

Negrito (neg-*ree*-to)—an aboriginal inhabitant of the Philippines, so-called from dark skin and kinky hair.

peso (*pay*-so)—the unit of Philippine currency, officially valued since 1962 at four to the United States dollar; divided into 100 centavos (sen-*tah*-vos).

Pilipino (pee-lee-*peen*-o)—the national language of the Philippine Republic: a simplified form of Tagalog which, in turn, is a form of the Malay language.

rajah (*rah*-jah)—in the old Moslem Philippines, a petty prince or chieftain, superior to a *cacique* or a *datu* in rank and wider in jurisdiction.

sari-sari store (sah-ree-sah-ree)—in the rural Philippines, a small general store stocked with consumer goods.

Tagalog (tah-*gah*-log)—the most widespread of native languages in the Philippines, a variant of Malay; also, a member of an important ethnic group living mostly in central Luzon.

tao (*tah*-o)—a poor farmer or farm laborer in the Philippines; in Tagalog, a man.

Thomasites—the 765 American school teachers who arrived in the Philippines on the army transport *Thomas* in 1901.

Visayas (vee-*sye*-as)—the islands in the middle of the Philippine archipelago between Luzon and Mindanao; the most important of them are Cebu, Bohol, Negros, Leyte, Panay and Samar.

Bibliography

This list includes important English-language sources published only in the Philippines. They are available in the United States at the largest libraries, notably the Library of Congress in Washington, but can be ordered through American bookshops that specialize in Asian materials.

Agoncillo, Teodoro A. and Alfonso, Oscar M. *A Short History of the Philippines* Quezon City: University of the Philippines, 1960
A nationalistic narrative, from prehistory to President García.

Beyer, H. Otley "The Philippines Before Magellan," *Asia* magazine, November 1921
The foremost ethnologist in the Philippines sums up what little is known about Hindu, Chinese, and other pre-Spanish influences.

——— *Population of the Philippine Islands in 1916* Manila: Philippine Education Co., Inc., 1917
Still useful for its descriptions of ethnographic groups.

Blair, Emma Helen, and Robertson, James Alexander (editors) *The Philippine Islands, 1493–1898* 55 volumes. Cleveland: The A. H. Clark Co., 1903–9
The richest treasure-house in English of basic historical documents; Volume II contains Antonio Pigafetta's journal of his voyage with Magellan.

Bowring, Sir John *A Visit to the Philippine Islands* London: Smith, Elder and Co., 1859
A British colonial official tells what it was like in the Islands toward the end of Spanish rule.

Forbes, William Cameron *The Philippine Islands* 2 volumes. Boston: Houghton Mifflin Co., 1928 (1-volume condensation, 1945)
A former governor general reviews the background and history of America's first thirty years as a colonial power in Asia.

234

Golay, Frank H. *The Philippines: Public Policy and National Economic Development* Ithaca, N. Y.: Cornell University Press, 1961
New light on the predicament of a poor-rich country.

Huke, Robert E. *Shadows on the Land: An Economic Geography of the Philippines* Manila: The Bookmark, Inc., 1963
Six Filipinos and one American contributed to this up-to-date survey.

Hunt, Chester L. and others *Sociology in the Philippine Setting* Quezon City: Phoenix Publishing House, revised edition, 1963
A basic textbook by six Filipinos and six Americans.

Pecson, Geronima T. and Racelis, Maria (editors) *Tales of the American Teachers in the Philippines* Manila: Carmelo & Bauermann, Inc., 1959 (paper)
Reminiscences of the devoted men and women who taught in the Islands in the early 1900's, forerunners of the Peace Corps teachers. One of the authors is a senator and the other is a sociologist.

Pelzer, Karl J. *Pioneer Settlement in the Asiatic Tropics* New York: American Geographical Society, 1945
A study of land use and land tenure in the Philippines and Java, contrasting the two colonial regimes against their historical backgrounds.

Phelan, John Leddy *The Hispanization of the Philippines: Spanish Aims and Filipino Responses, 1565–1700* Madison, Wisconsin: The University of Wisconsin Press, 1959
A compact, scholarly account, sympathetic to Spain and the Roman Catholic church.

Purcell, Victor *The Chinese in Southeast Asia* London: Oxford University Press, 1965 (revised edition)
The last 73 pages of this monumental work deal in detail with the history, condition, and prospects of the Chinese minority in the Philippines.

Ravenholt, Albert *The Philippines, a Young Republic on the Move* Princeton, New Jersey: D. Van Nostrand Company, Inc., 1962
A friendly appraisal of the independent Philippines by a seasoned American correspondent, a contributor to the American University Field Staff reports, who has lived in the Islands for many years.

Report to the President of the United States by the Economic Mission to the Philippines Washington: Government Printing Office, 1950
The famous Bell Report, which sounded an alarm and called for drastic reforms.

Rivera, G. F., and McMillan, R. T. *The Rural Philippines* Manila: Mutual Security Agency, 1952
A study of social and economic problems of the village people, with suggested lines of action.

Rizal, José *The Lost Eden (Noli Me Tangere)* Bloomington, Indiana: Indiana University Press, 1961
A new translation, by Leon M. Guerrero, of the novel that helped to spark the Filipino revolution against Spain.

Romulo, Carlos P. *Crusade in Asia: Philippine Victory* New York: The John Day Company, 1955
An account of the Huk insurrection and of Magsaysay's triumph.

Romulo, Carlos P. *I Walked with Heroes* New York: Holt, Rinehart and Winston, Inc., 1961
Personal recollections by the Philippine Republic's most effective advocate abroad, the first Asian to become President of the United Nations General Assembly.

Saleeby, Najeeb M. *The History of Sulu* Manila: Filipiniana Book Guild, Inc., 1963
The outstanding work on Moro history and lore, originally written in 1908.

Schurz, William Lytle   *The Manila Galleon*   New York: E. P. Dutton & Co., Inc., 1939 (paper, 1959)
   The grandeurs and miseries of the sailing ships that brought the riches of the East to Mexico, and thus to Spain.

Taylor, George E.   *The Philippines and the United States: Problems of Partnership*   New York: Frederick A. Praeger, 1964
   An expert in Far Eastern history describes and appraises the political, economic, and military relationships between the two countries; a valuable study.

Zaide, Gregorio F.   *Philippine History for High Schools*   Manila: The Modern Book Company, 1962
   Useful for American readers because of its detailed treatment of the pre-Spanish and Spanish periods; friendly both to the Roman Catholic Church and to Philippine nationalism.

Too numerous to list here are the American histories, biographies and memoirs of the 1898–1946 epoch of American control. A few notable examples are *In the Days of McKinley,* by Margaret Leech; *Splendid Little War,* by Frank Freidel; *Little Brown Brother,* by Leon Wolff (on the "Philippine insurrection"); Volume I of *The Life and Times of William Howard Taft,* by Henry F. Pringle; and *On Active Service in Peace and War,* by Henry L. Stimson and McGeorge Bundy. The American military histories and personal memoirs about World War II in the Philippines would fill a small library.

Credits

The format for *The Philippines* was designed by Robert Sugar. The cover was prepared by Leah Ice. The maps were drawn by Donald T. Pitcher.

For the photographs on the following pages we gratefully credit:

Appendix

American Governors-General of the Philippines

1901–1904	William Howard Taft
1904–1906	Luke E. Wright
1906	Henry C. Ide
1906–1909	James F. Smith
1909–1913	W. Cameron Forbes
1913–1921	Francis Burton Harrison
1921–1927	Leonard Wood
1928–1929	Henry L. Stimson
1929–1932	Dwight F. Davis
1932–1933	Theodore Roosevelt, Jr.
1933–1935	Frank Murphy

Presidents of the Philippines

Under the Commonwealth

1935–1944	Manuel L. Quezon*
1944–1946	Sergio Osmeña
1946	Manuel A. Roxas

Under the Republic

1946–1948	Manuel A. Roxas*
1948–1953	Elpidio Quirino
1953–1957	Ramón Magsaysay*
1957–1961	Carlos P. Garcia
1961–1965	Diosdado Macapagal
1965–	Ferdinand E. Marcos

* died in office

Index

DATE DUE